GREAT HISTORIC DISASTERS

THE
HINDENBURG
DISASTER OF 1937

GREAT HISTORIC DISASTERS

GREAT HISTORIC DISASTERS

THE
HINDENBURG
DISASTER OF 1937

WILLIAM W. LACE

CHELSEA HOUSE
PUBLISHERS
An imprint of Infobase Publishing

Chelsea House
An imprint of Infobase Publishing
132 West 31st Street
New York, NY 10001

Library of Congress Cataloging-in-Publication Data
Lace, William W.
The Hindenburg disaster of 1937/William W. Lace.
   p.   cm.—(Great historic disasters)
Includes bibliographical references.
ISBN: 978-0-7910-9739-7 (hardcover)
1. Hindenburg (Airship) 2. Aircraft accidents—New Jersey. 3. Airships—Germany. I. Title. II. Series.
TL659.H5L23 2008
363.12'465—dc22   2008004890

Chelsea House books are available at special discounts when purchased in bulk quantities for businesses, associations, institutions, or sales promotions. Please call our Special Sales Department in New York at (212) 967-8800 or (800) 322-8755.

You can find Chelsea House on the World Wide Web
at http://www.chelseahouse.com

Text design by Annie O'Donnell
Cover design by Ben Peterson

Printed in the United States of America

Bang KT 10 9 8 7 6 5 4 3 2 1

This book is printed on acid-free paper.

All links and Web addresses were checked and verified to be correct at the time of publication. Because of the dynamic nature of the Web, some addresses and links may have changed since publication and may no longer be valid.

Contents

Introduction: Approach

At long last, the thunderstorms moved away from New Jersey's Lakehurst Naval Air Station. All day long on Thursday, May 6, 1937, people had "crowded around the airport like a pack of hungry wolves," passenger Leonhard Adelt later wrote in *Reader's Digest*. They were there to witness the landing of the *Hindenburg*, a celebrated dirigible (balloon-like airship). Surface winds, which had been more than 25 miles per hour, slacked off to a gentle breeze. As later reported by the *New York Times*, Commander Charles E. Rosendahl, the station chief, sent a message to the giant airship: "Conditions definitely improved recommend earliest possible landing."

Captain Max Pruss, commanding officer of the *Hindenburg*, received the message with relief. It had been more than two hours since the airship first sighted Lakehurst's tall mast, at which it was to dock after the transatlantic flight from Germany. However, the weather had made landing impossible. Furthermore, the *Hindenburg* should have landed that morning, but headwinds over the ocean had delayed the journey.

It was not that Pruss was worried about running out of fuel. The zeppelin could cruise for days more if need be, held aloft by 16 giant bags filled with buoyant—yet highly flammable— hydrogen gas. After all, its sister ship, the *Graf Zeppelin*, had once circled above Buenos Aires for five days while revolutionaries battled the Argentine army below. However, the *Hindenburg's* flight plan had called for a quick turnaround, and there were only a few hours scheduled before passengers would board for the return trip. A sign outside the fence apologetically told the public that there could be no visits to the ship because of the tight schedule. There would not even be time, Pruss wired, to wait for the dirty sheets and towels to be laundered and returned.

The delay was also an annoyance to chief steward Heinrich Kubis, who was responsible for the passengers' comfort. Those passengers had not eaten since lunch and would soon be hungry. Kubis ordered one of his stewards, Eugen Nunnenmacher, to begin making sandwiches. The dining room, rearranged for U.S. customs inspectors, would have to be set up again.

Food was also on the minds of many of the men waiting on the ground to help with the landing. It took 232 men hauling on ropes to ease the huge craft—804 feet long and 135 feet across at the widest point—down to its berth at the foot of the mast. Since there were not enough Navy-enlisted men at Lakehurst to make up the crew, civilians had to be recruited from neighboring towns. Twice the crew had been called to their positions only to be soaked by passing showers. It was past time for the sailors' supper, and this only added to their misery. The townsmen felt a little better. At least they were getting paid a dollar an hour, and some of them, like Allen Hagaman, had brought food with them. Watching from beyond the fence was Hagaman's 15-year-old daughter, Sarah.

HERBERT MORRISON

While the ground crew had been on hand only a few hours, Herbert Morrison had spent all day waiting for the *Hindenburg* to arrive. The young broadcaster from Chicago station WLS had set up his equipment in a small shack with a good

Before airplanes became a popular method of travel, dirigibles were used to shuttle people over oceans and continents. These airships gave passengers a bird's-eye view of the world, and a faster means of transportation than ocean liners. However, this method hardly had a chance to catch on, due to the tragedy of the *Hindenburg*, which effectively ended passenger travel by dirigible.

view of the field. American Airlines, which had begun a schedule of flights to allow zeppelin passengers to fly to cities in the Midwest, had arranged for his trip.

Aboard the airship, Joseph Späh was also impatient. The German-born comedian, whose stage name was Ben Dova, was returning from a successful series of performances in Europe. His wife and three children, whom he had not seen for weeks, were waiting at Lakehurst, and he was due to open a new act at New York's Radio City Music Hall in a few days. He took advantage of the delay to go to the cargo hold to pay one more visit to Ulla, a four-month-old, purebred German shepherd dog intended as a present for his children.

For some of the *Hindenburg* passengers, however, the extra hours in the air were a bonus—more time in which to enjoy the view from the windows lining the promenade on one side and the lounge on the other. Weather had constantly interfered with their aerial sightseeing, and Leonhard Adelt called the trip "the most uneventful journey I ever took on an airship."

Now, however, the passengers circled over cities and towns. They could see deer, startled by the sight of the giant ship, bounding into the woods. Margaret Mather, a veteran world traveler born in New Jersey but living in Rome, pointed out landmarks to her fellow passengers. "I was feeling foolish with happiness and didn't really care how long this cruising lasted," she later wrote in *Harper's Monthly Magazine*.

George Grant was too much of a veteran zeppelin traveler to do much window gazing. The assistant manager of the airship company's London office sat in the lounge and wrote in his diary, as recounted in *The Hindenburg* by Michael Mooney, "The *Hindenburg* is likely to go to posterity as a forerunner of regular worldwide travel by airship."

Waiting was also no problem for Arthur Johnson, the New York City police detective assigned to be on the lookout for possible spies slipping into the country from Adolf Hitler's Nazi Germany. To pass the time, he read the latest issue of *Collier's* magazine, which contained a story about the German zeppelin fleet. The story's author, W.B. Courtney, wrote, "German dirigibles have flown nearly one million passengers without a fatality. And . . . only a stroke of war or an unfathomable act of God will ever mar this German dirigible passenger safety record."

MORRISON'S BROADCAST

Finally, the waiting was at an end, and the *Hindenburg* glided majestically toward the mooring mast. Herbert Morrison, as quoted in Rick Archbold's *Hindenburg*, began his broadcast:

Here it comes, ladies and gentlemen, and what a sight it is, a thrilling one, just a marvelous sight. . . . The mighty diesel motors roar, the propellers biting into the air and throwing it back into gale-like whirlpools. . . . No one wonders that this great floating palace can travel through the air at such speed with these powerful motors behind it. The sun is striking the windows of the observation deck on the eastward side and sparkling like glittering jewels against a background of black velvet.

At an altitude of 360 feet, chief engineer Rudolf Sauter reported that the ship was slightly tail-heavy. Pruss corrected by dumping more than 2,000 pounds of water kept in the stern tanks for just that purpose and sent six extra men into the bow, or front, for extra weight. The *Hindenburg* was now "level as a board," Captain Heinrich Bauer was quoted as saying, in A.A. Hoehling's book *Who Destroyed the Hindenburg?*

At an altitude of 200 feet, first the landing lines were dropped. The ropes smacked into the earth below and were quickly snared by the ground crew. At 7:24 P.M., the wind began to pick up, caus- ing the crew members to dig in their heels to hold the *Hindenburg* in place. Then, suddenly, all was quiet. Adelt wrote that

there occurred a remarkable stillness. . . . It seemed as though the whole world was holding its breath. One heard no command, no call, no cry. The people we saw [on the ground] seemed suddenly stiffened. I could not account for this. Then, I heard a light, dull detonation from above, no louder than the sound of a beer bottle being opened.

A few moments later, the *Hindenburg* lay in ruins. And with it, all hopes or dreams of a vast fleet of dirgibles.

1

LZ129

When the *Hindenburg* left Germany on its fateful voyage, it was the largest, longest, and most luxurious aircraft ever to fly. Count Ferdinand Adolf August Heinrich von Zeppelin was the man whose dreams and determination made the trip possible. His contributions were recognized even in the official designation of the *Hindenburg*: LZ129, LZ standing for *Luftschiffe* (Airship) *Zeppelin*.

Zeppelin's passion for aircraft began on August 19, 1863, 80 years after the Montgolfier brothers sent the first hot air balloon skyward over the fields of southern France. Zeppelin, a 25-year-old officer in the service of the king of the German state of Württemberg, had used his family influence to wrangle an assignment to the United States as a Civil War observer. He had seen balloons being used by the Union army for reconnaissance but had not been permitted to go on a flight.

Two months later, wishing to see the American frontier, he made his way up the Mississippi River to St. Paul, Minnesota, where he found a more accommodating balloon operator. With the other passengers, he soared to an altitude of 700 feet—the length of the tether rope—and looked at the countryside below.

While others might have been spellbound by the breathtaking view, Zeppelin had a more practical, military turn of mind. He imagined himself commanding an army that was attacking an enemy force dug in on a ridge of hills he could see to the west. He wrote to his father later that day, as quoted in Rick Archbold's *Hindenburg*, "No method is better suited to viewing quickly the terrain of an unknown, enemy-occupied position."

THE BALLOON IN WARTIME

Seven years later, in 1870, Zeppelin saw a practical application of his observation while serving with the German army at the siege of Paris during the Franco-Prussian War. The French used balloons not only for observation but also to send messages between troops inside and outside the city. Four years later, the count wrote in his diary a remarkably accurate prediction of what a dirigible—an airship that could be controlled and guided as opposed to a balloon—would eventually be. Archbold quotes him as writing that it should have a rigid frame, and "the gas compartment should, whenever possible, be divided into cells which can be filled and emptied individually."

There had been significant airship developments in the 10 years after Zeppelin's initial balloon ride. Hot air had largely been replaced by hydrogen gas, and hydrogen called for an airtight bag rather than one with an opening at the bottom because the gas, when mixed with air or oxygen, is highly flammable.

Airtight bags, in turn, presented difficulties of their own. The higher the craft rose, the more the gas inside expanded because of a decrease in surrounding air pressure. Also, with no way to decrease the volume of gas, there was no way to make the craft descend. After a French duke had to poke a hole in his balloon to keep it from exploding at high altitude, valves were invented so that gas could be "valved off."

Zeppelin had to put aside his airship ambitions because of his duties as a soldier, but they were rekindled in 1884 when the dirigible *La France* was flown by two French balloon corps officers. Its electric motor could generate a speed of only 14 miles per hour, and the batteries were quickly drained.

CHALLENGER TO GERMANY

The French press, however, made much of *La France*'s flight. Zeppelin, ever mindful of possible military applications of airships, wrote to the king of Württemberg, as quoted by Archbold, saying that Germany should answer the French challenge by building airships "to carry personnel, cargo, or explosive shells." Such views, however, were not popular with the German high command, dominated by officers from Prussia, another German state. They resented what they considered interference by an outsider and managed to force Zeppelin to resign from the army in 1890.

Zeppelin now had time to pursue his dream of building an airship and, thanks to his inherited family fortune, the money to make it come true. Two developments came to his aid. The first had already taken place when, in 1886, Gottlieb Daimler perfected the gasoline engine. Such engines would be light and powerful enough to propel an airship. The first such ship, however—designed in 1897 by another German team—exploded in midair, a victim of a gas leak and an exposed flame on the Daimler engine.

Another unsuccessful aircraft, also in 1897, provided the second development. Carl Berg, who had recently succeeded in manufacturing aluminum in commercial quantities, teamed with David Schwarz to create a ship made of the ultralight metal. The ship crashed shortly after liftoff, but Zeppelin was impressed with the possibilities of aluminum and went into partnership with Berg the next year to form an airship manufacturing company.

FLIGHT OF THE LZ1

Two years later, on July 2, 1900, the white-haired count, now 62 years old, stood at the controls of the LZ1. The airship,

Ferdinand von Zeppelin *(above)* believed that hot air balloons, which were used in warfare for reconnaissance, could be converted into attack vehicles. After combining a hot air balloon, a gas-powered engine, and air valves, Zeppelin created a dirigible with a rigid frame that could fly instead of float. His invention would lead to the production of zeppelins, including the *Hindenburg*, to be used for civilian transportation.

looking somewhat like a 425-foot wiener, was towed on a barge from its hangar to the middle of Lake Constance near the picturesque town of Friedrichshafen. The towropes were cast off, the two four-cylinder Daimler engines were started, and the LZ1 rose majestically to 1,300 feet and began to lazily circle the lake.

The crowd, virtually the entire population of the town, cheered, but not for long. Eighteen minutes into the flight, the rudder controls tangled and the framework buckled. Fortunately, the LZ1 was able to land gently near the shore, but it could not avoid a stake that punctured one of the gas cells.

Two more flights were more successful, but not to the extent that the army would offer a contract for future construction. Zeppelin's company was out of money, but he persuaded the king to organize a state lottery to bring in money for another attempt. Five years later, the LZ2 was able to reach a speed of 25 miles per hour. However, it proved to be unmaneuverable and crash-landed.

Undaunted, the count went on to build the LZ3, which made an eight-hour flight in 1907. The next year, an improved model, the LZ4, made a 12-hour round-trip to Switzerland. Zeppelin was acclaimed a hero throughout Germany, and plans were made for a 24-hour endurance flight that, if successful, would result in an army contract. The first part of the journey went well, but shortly after the ship had been forced to land with engine problems, a sudden storm tore it loose and slammed it into a tree, whereupon it burst into flames.

SUPPORT FROM THE PEOPLE

Count Zeppelin thought the destruction of the LZ4 had destroyed his airship aspirations as well, but the German people had other ideas. They adopted Zeppelin and his airship program as a matter of national pride. Contributions came in from all parts of the country. Schoolchildren sent in pennies.

Some farmers who had little money donated food. Before long, more than 6 million marks, about $1.4 million, had been collected, an enormous sum for a time in which an average worker in the United States might earn $600 per year.

The influx of money enabled Zeppelin to build the LZ5 and LZ6, which public opinion almost forced the army to buy. The military, however, eventually preferred a design from August von Parseval, a competitor, and the count had to look elsewhere. Fortunately he had engaged Alfred Colsman as business manager and former journalist Hugo Eckener as public relations director, and the pair convinced the count, somewhat against his will, to make airships for passenger instead of military use.

Hugo Eckener

Hugo Eckener, who eventually managed the Zeppelin company, had earlier, as a journalist, criticized the airship. He covered the second flight of the LZ1 in 1900, writing for the *Frankfurter Zeitung* newspaper. He had this to say, as quoted by Rick Archbold in *Hindenburg*:

> There was no question of the airship flying for any appreciable distance or hovering at various altitudes. One had the feeling that they were very happy to balance up there so nicely, and indeed the fine equilibrium of the airship was the most successful aspect of the whole affair. But under what circumstances were the modest results, which I have described, achieved? Under the best possible conditions—an almost complete calm.

The idea was received enthusiastically across Germany, many cities building zeppelin hangars at their own expense, long in advance of any scheduled service. It would be 1910 before the Deutsche Luftschiffahrts-Aktien-Gesellschaft (DELAG), or German Airship Transport Company, provided the first flight with paying passengers. Unfortunately, the aircraft, the LZ7 *Deutschland*, loaded with reporters in addition to passengers, had to make a forced landing and was wrecked. The LZ8 *Deutschland II* also had problems, and it was not until 1911 and the LZ10 *Schwaben* that zeppelin travel became popular and profitable.

ONBOARD LUXURY

The *Schwaben* provided a foretaste of what was to come on the *Hindenburg*. There were as yet no sleeping quarters—the journeys between German cities were too brief—but passengers rode in a gondola, a compartment just below the ship's body, that provided all the luxuries of a first-class railroad carriage. Paneling was mahogany, with mother-of-pearl inlays. A washroom, including a toilet, was available. Passengers could watch the view below through broad windows while eating pâté, cold chicken, caviar, and ham—all washed down with champagne, port, and sherry.

The *Schwaben* proved hugely popular and was quickly followed by the *Viktoria Luise*, *Hansa*, and *Sachsen*. More than 34,000 passengers flew more than 100,000 miles without a serious mishap until 1914, when the outbreak of World War I changed everything.

Almost overnight, Count Zeppelin's original vision for the airship became a reality. Suddenly, his company could not build enough zeppelins for the army and navy. And, as often happens under the pressures of war, they grew larger, swifter, and sturdier than they would have in peacetime.

The wartime zeppelins proved adept, not only for scouting and reconnaissance, but also for attack. But, just as the war

Like the *Titanic* before it, the *Hindenburg* was to be the biggest and best of its kind—the largest airship in history with the most luxurious travel accommodations. After four and a half years of construction, the completed *Hindenburg* measured 800 feet long and 135 feet wide, and was able to carry 36 tons.

accelerated German zeppelin technology, it also gave a boost to the British aircraft industry. "Height climbers" that could reach 25,000 feet were developed. They carried machine guns loaded with incendiary phosphorus bullets that, when piercing the zeppelin's skin, ignited the hydrogen. On September 2, 1916, and again on October 1, British planes reduced attacking zeppelins to balls of flame.

The days of the zeppelin as a war machine had effectively ended, and one person who saw this most clearly was Count Zeppelin, now 78 years old but still able to ride on new aircraft and to pester the German high command to return him to active duty. Yet, he realized that the future of aerial war belonged to airplanes. Accordingly, he established a company that succeeded in building planes capable of carrying a 2,000-pound bomb.

DEATH OF COUNT ZEPPELIN

Count Zeppelin, however, would not live to see his last success. He fell ill at an aeronautical exhibition in Berlin in February 1917 and died of pneumonia in March of that year. As his coffin was lowered into the grave, two zeppelins draped in black dropped flowers onto the mourners.

After the war, the count's company, the Luftschiffbau Zeppelin, planned to resume its successful passenger service. The success would not last long. The victorious allies were determined to punish Germany, and part of the punishment was that all aircraft—including zeppelins—were to be transferred to Britain, France, and Italy. Some workers destroyed aircraft in their hangars rather than see them be handed over.

So it was that during the 1920s, while Luftschiffbau Zeppelin barely kept in business making aluminum pots and pans, other countries sought to increase their airship manufacturing. Their attempts were largely unsuccessful and frequently ended in disaster. The Italian-built *Roma*, the British R-34, and the American *Shenandoah*—all military craft—crashed, claiming 58 lives. When 48 passengers and crew members of Britain's R-101 were killed in 1930, the British canceled plans for more airships.

Meanwhile, the Zeppelin company had worked its way back into the airship business by building the LZ126 *Los Angeles* for the U.S. Navy in 1922. Eventually, the *Los Angeles*'s success (and the lack of success by other countries) opened the door to construction of a German aircraft for Germany. On September 18, 1928, the LZ127, christened the *Graf Zeppelin* by the count's daughter, made its maiden flight.

THE GRAF ZEPPELIN

The *Graf Zeppelin* was 775 feet long and was borne aloft by more than 3 million cubic feet of hydrogen. Its maximum speed was 105 miles per hour, and a transatlantic crossing could be made in 60 hours as compared to 125 for an ocean liner.

And Eckener did his best to ensure that the *Graf Zeppelin* compared favorably to an ocean liner in terms of comfort and luxury. The gondola's passenger quarters, designed for multiple-day travel, contained 10 two-person cabins with bunk beds, each cabin having an exterior window. There were shared washrooms and toilets but, as yet, no bathing facilities.

The small dining room did double duty as a lounge, and—over the objections of Dürr, who feared the possibility of a fire—there was a complete kitchen capable of preparing and serving hot meals. One enjoyment the gentlemen passengers missed, however, was an after-dinner cigar. Smoking was strictly forbidden because of the threat of fire and the proximity of tons of explosive hydrogen.

The *Graf Zeppelin*, which made its first U.S. trip in October 1928, was a huge success with the public, but Eckener was having trouble attracting the money needed to build airships even larger and grander. The *Graf Zeppelin* carried only 20 passengers, and greater capacity was needed in order to make flights profitable. He sought more publicity by arranging the first passenger flight around the world in 1929—a feat accomplished in only 22 days—but the Great Depression was just around the corner, and investors would become scarce.

THE NAZIS AS PARTNERS

When investors did appear, however, they were not the type Eckener would have preferred. Adolf Hitler and the Nazis had come to power in 1933, and the *Graf Zeppelin* now bore large, black swastikas, the Nazi symbol. Hitler's propaganda minister, Joseph Goebbels, saw the value of such publicity and personally contributed more than $500,000 toward the building of a new airship. And air minister Hermann Göring, even though he held what he called "gasbags" in contempt, came up with more than $2 million. Another $2.2 million came from the government-supported Lufthansa airline, and the result was a new public-private company—the Deutsche Zeppelin-Reederei, or German Zeppelin Transport Company, usually referred to simply as the Redeerei.

Eckener had a low opinion of his new partners, but it was Nazi money that would make it possible to build what authors Harold Dick and Douglas Robinson, in *Graf Zeppelin* and *Hindenburg*, called "Eckener's dream of the ideal transatlantic ship." The first step—after a large enough hangar was constructed—was to use more than 10 miles of Duralumin, an aluminum/copper alloy, to build 16 giant rings, the largest of which was 135 feet high, equal to a 14-story building, and hang them in a horizontal line parallel to one another at specific intervals. The rings were then connected by a series of 36 girders stretching from bow to stern a total of 804 feet—more than four times the length of the nonrigid "blimps" now commonly seen above U.S. sporting events and only 78 feet shorter than the ocean liner *Titanic*. When all were connected, Mooney wrote, the effect was like "the skeleton of some fantastic whale."

The 16 rings divided the LZ129 into compartments, each containing a gas cell. The bags were made of cotton and made gastight with a new kind of lining—layers of cloth cemented to either side of a layer of celluloid somewhat like photographic film. Each bag was separated from its neighbor by a cotton partition and was held in place by netting and lines to keep it from rubbing against any metal surfaces. A special coating was applied to reflect the heat of the Sun coming through the outer skin.

When fully inflated, the 16 bags held a total of 7.2 million cubic feet of gas. That gas, however, would turn out to be hydrogen. The ship had been designed for helium, which is nonflammable but has less lifting power than hydrogen. The only large sources of helium, however, were in the United States, and export of the gas was forbidden under federal law, since the U.S. government did not want to help any foreign power build aircraft that might be used for war.

There was some disagreement within the Redeerei about which gas was preferable. Eckener preferred helium. Not only was it safer, he thought, but to buy it from the United States would earn them the goodwill of the Americans. Captain Ernst Lehmann pointed to the superior lifting power of hydrogen, the fact that no serious mishaps had taken place, and to the high cost of helium—$80 per 1,000 cubic feet as compared to about $4 for hydrogen.

The outer skin of the zeppelin was cotton coated on the outside with silver paint designed to reflect sunlight. The top part of the inside of the skin was painted red to help block the Sun's ultraviolet rays.

Two exterior pods on either side of the LZ129 held 16-cylinder diesel engines—the first used on zeppelins—capable of generating a total of 5,000 horsepower. Normal cruising speed was about 80 miles per hour, and the ship had a range of about 10,000 miles.

The ship was operated from a 9-foot-by 28-foot gondola on the underside. The steering compartment held two wheels— one for the helmsman who controlled the vertical rudders that

As one of Zeppelin's earliest associates in aeronautics, Hugo Eckener *(above)* played a significant role in promoting, designing, and flying the airships. Eckener's around-the-world trips gave the zeppelins international exposure, and attracted investors to fund the company's dream vehicle, a ship that would eventually be called the *Hindenburg*.

moved the ship right or left and another for the "elevator man," whose horizontal rudders, the elevators, controlled vertical movement. There were also gauges giving readings on cell pressure and controls for releasing either gas to make the ship descend or water ballast to make it rise.

The design change that set the LZ129 apart from its predecessors was that everything else—passenger and crew quarters, kitchen, dining rooms, washrooms, cargo hold—was inside the main body of the ship rather than in a gondola. "B Deck," just above the control gondola, held two innovations—a shower and a smoking room. The smoking room was entered through the small, 24-hour bar, and the door was controlled by a bar steward whose job it was to see that no smoking materials—especially matches—were carried into other parts of the ship.

Passenger cabins were functional—two bunk beds, the bottom of which could be made into a sofa, and a washbasin. Unlike the *Graf Zeppelin*, most of the cabins had no windows, but both the lounge and dining room that faced outside on either side of the cabins had large banks of windows that could even be opened in fair weather. Both the lounge and dining room had well-upholstered chairs and tasteful murals on the walls. The lounge boasted a baby grand piano, made largely of aluminum to save weight.

THE MAIDEN FLIGHT

The LZ129 made its first flight—a three-hour trial run with Eckener aboard and Captain Lehmann commanding—on March 4, 1936. The next day, a longer flight went over the city of Munich, whose mayor asked Eckener by radio what the name of the ship was. "*Hindenburg*" was the answer.

On landing, Eckener received a summons to Goebbels's Berlin office. The Nazi propaganda minister had wanted the LZ129 named the *Adolf Hitler* and was furious that Eckener had, without consulting him, chosen to honor the memory of Paul von Hindenburg, German's supreme military commander in World War I and Hitler's immediate predecessor as president. Since Eckener had made his choice public, it could not be easily retracted. Goebbels told Eckener, however, that the ship would be known in the German news media only as the LZ129.

One of the next flights of the *Hindenburg* would be one of the most controversial. On March 7, Hitler had sent German troops into the Rhineland region in violation of the postwar Treaty of Versailles. He called a national referendum for March 29, asking the German people whether they approved

More Engaging than Hitler

One of the *Hindenburg*'s earliest and most controversial flights came in March 1936 when the airship and its sister ship, *Graf Zeppelin*, were ordered to drop leaflets urging Germans to support the army's march into the Rhineland. It was by no means, however, the airship's only propaganda flight.

In August of that year, Nazi propaganda minister Joseph Goebbels thought that it would be symbolic of German power for the *Hindenburg* to appear over Berlin's Olympias- tadion for the opening ceremonies of the Olympic Games. The ship proved to be such an awe-inspiring sight that most of the 100,000 people there seemed to be paying more attention to it than to German chancellor Adolf Hitler. It was rumored, according to Michael Mooney's *The Hindenburg*, that the Nazi leader was so annoyed that he brusquely ordered, *"Hindenburg Auf!"* (*"Hindenburg* away!")

or not. The Air Ministry ordered the *Graf Zeppelin* and *Hindenburg* to fly over cities dropping leaflets urging support of the Nazi leader. Eckener had no choice but to comply.

When the *Hindenburg* was towed out of its hangar, however, a sudden wind gust slammed it into the ground, damaging a fin. Lehmann ordered quick repairs to be made so that the flight could continue. Eckener objected strenuously and publicly, shouting at Lehmann, Archbold quoted, that he was risking the ship for "this idiotic flight."

A few days later, after the first transatlantic flight landed in Rio de Janeiro, Eckener learned that not only the *Hindenburg*'s name, but also his own, had been barred. Goebbels had decreed, as quoted by Mooney, that "The name of Dr. Hugo Eckener will no longer be mentioned in newspapers and periodicals. No pictures nor articles about him shall be printed."

Despite the displeasure of the Nazis, Eckener's name was at the top of the crew list on the first flight to New York City on May 6, although Lehmann was listed as "commander." The passenger list included two German counts, three members of the British nobility, a noted explorer, and a mystery novelist. There was even a priest, Father Paul Schulte, who had special permission from Pope Pius XI to conduct a service on board.

ARRIVAL IN NEW YORK

Even though it was barely dawn when the *Hindenburg* reached New York, thousands of people stood in Times Square, cheering when the ship turned its searchlight on them. After the landing at Lakehurst, Eckener and Lehmann went first to New York for a German-American Chamber of Commerce dinner and the next day to Washington, D.C., to meet President Franklin D. Roosevelt. Eckener tried to get the president to agree to lift the embargo on helium. Roosevelt was noncommittal.

The *Hindenburg* made 10 round-trips to the United States in 1936, but because winter weather over the North Atlantic made more trips to North America impossible, the *Hindenburg* spent those months on the Germany-Brazil run. Plans were announced, however, for even more American flights in 1937. The first was scheduled for Monday, May 3.

2 "Up Ship!"

As the *Hindenburg* **was prepared for its first** North American flight of the 1937 season, passengers and crew alike felt the usual sense of excitement and anticipation. Beneath the joviality, however, was a nagging feeling of disquiet. Security precautions had been unusually strict. Nazi Germany had many enemies, and unknown persons had tried to sabotage zeppelins in the recent past. Would they try again?

The Germans had ample cause for concern. Two years earlier, a routine inspection revealed a time bomb hidden beneath a chair in the main lounge of the *Graf Zeppelin*. Then, only a few months past, a passenger on the *Hindenburg*'s final flight from South America began asking questions that made the crew suspicious. After the flight, the *Geheime Staatspolizei*, or gestapo, searched the man's hotel room. They found diagrams of the *Hindenburg* and *Graf Zeppelin*, but the man had disappeared.

There were threats and warnings, many of them coming from the United States. "I have repeatedly received anonymous letters warning the *Hindenburg* not to land at Lakehurst," Eckener wrote to the German Air Ministry, according to Archbold.

At least one letter of warning was not anonymous. Less than a month before, Dr. Hans Luther, Germany's ambassador to the United States, received a letter from a woman in Milwaukee, Wisconsin, named Kathie Rauch. It read, in part, as quoted by A.A. Hoehling, that the *Hindenburg*

> is going to be destroyed by a time bomb during its flight to another country. While I cannot explain the secrecy of this, please believe my words as the truth, so that no one later will have cause for regret. . . . Later I can send you a clearer report.

WARNING PASSED ALONG

Luther routinely sent such letters to the Foreign Office in Berlin, but this one seemed to be authentic. He singled it out from the rest, and it was eventually passed on to the *Schutzstaffel*, or SS—German for "Protective Squadron"—and on to the Redeerei.

Rumors of such threats naturally spread throughout the Redeerei, so it was probably no surprise that on Sunday, May 2, crewmen approaching the *Hindenburg*'s enormous hangar at Frankfurt's Flughafen airport saw a line of troopers from the *Sicherheitsdienst*, or SD, the security branch of the SS. The troops stood at parade rest, automatic rifles across their chests.

The senior crewman, chief rigger Ludwig Knorr, approached the officer in charge, who was talking with zeppelin captain Anton Wittemann. Wittemann explained that the SS had ordered a complete inspection of the *Hindenburg*. Division chiefs, such as Knorr, were to take two SD men to search their specific areas of responsibility.

Knorr, of course, had to agree. Privately, however, he thought the search was a waste of time that could be better spent readying the ship. A zeppelin man could hide a bomb in any of hundreds of places that a soldier would miss, and it was foolish, Knorr thought, to think a crew member would sabotage a ship he was to fly on.

A FRUITLESS SEARCH

Nevertheless, the search went forward—the SD men wearing cloth shoes instead of their usual hobnailed boots, which might strike sparks. The crewmen led them up stairways and along gangways. They searched every compartment—cabins, toilets, cargo areas, the control gondola, the kitchen. At least

Despite disagreeing with their principles and actions, Hugo Eckener had no choice but to accept the Nazi Party's financial assistance in building his airships. In return, he was forced to comply with certain demands, such as painting large swastikas on his airships (*above*) and using the *Hindenburg* to drop Nazi propaganda over Germany.

one area, however, went unsearched. The 16 giant gas cells had been fully inflated. There was no way, short of emptying them, to check the inside.

The search was the subject of much laughter later that evening when many members of the crew gathered for a farewell dinner in Frankfurt's Heldenkeller restaurant. The men emptied steins of beer and told stories about one another.

Knorr and the others refrained from poking too much fun at the ignorance and ineptness of the SD men who had searched the *Hindenburg*. After all, some of the crewmen were part of the Nazi Party and one, helmsman Helmut Lau, was a sergeant in the SS.

ERICH SPEHL

One of the couples gathered around the table with Knorr was rigger Erich Spehl and his girlfriend. Spehl was a relative newcomer to the crew. A former saddler's apprentice, he had joined the Redeerei in 1933 sewing gas cells and segments of the outer covering. Knorr took a liking to the 24-year-old and in 1936 made him part of the *Hindenburg*'s crew.

Quiet and moody, Spehl generally kept to himself and had few friends among his colleagues, except for a relationship with Knorr almost like son and father. Some, such as Lau, thought he was "odd." He appeared to have only one hobby—photography—and his apartment held a full darkroom, including timing devices.

Spehl's other passion was his girlfriend, who he had only known for a few weeks. She was six years older than Spehl and had been married twice. For most of the past year, she had been living with a man who introduced her to his circle of friends, which included leftists and members of Germany's Communist Party, bitter enemies of the Nazis. After her lover was killed in Spain fighting the Nazi-backed side in the civil war, she continued to be seen with anti-Hitler activists and introduced Spehl to them. Their activities were noticed both by Spehl's colleagues and by the SS.

The party broke up fairly early. After all, there was still much to do before liftoff the following evening. Most of the bachelors went to the ship. There, to their surprise and pleasure, they found they had been joined by Captain Lehmann.

A SUDDEN DECISION

Lehmann, the most experienced zeppelin man in the world besides Eckener, had received Kathie Rauch's letter. It had weighed on his mind, and he decided, only the day before, to accompany the *Hindenburg* to Lakehurst. He had in mind a visit to Washington to try to get the embargo on helium lifted, but his main purpose was simply to be with the crew—most of whom he had trained—at this unsettled time.

He came aboard carrying only a small suitcase and an accordion case. He was greeted by chief steward Kubis, who

The Lucky Ones

Several people may have owed their lives to the fact that, for one reason or another, they did not travel on the last flight of the *Hindenburg* as they had originally planned. The most famous at the time was Max Schmeling, the former world heavyweight boxing champion who the previous year had been the first person to defeat American Joe Louis.

Another non-passenger was correspondent William Shirer, who later authored *The Rise and Fall of the Third Reich*. Since the *Hindenburg* had only half its full number of passengers, Eckener—always seeking more publicity—invited Shirer and other journalists to fly free of charge. Shirer declined, as quoted in A.A. Hoehling's *Who Destroyed the Hindenburg?*, "for reasons which are a little obscure."

noted his lack of luggage. Lehmann said, quoted by Hoehling, "Kubis, I thought my being on board would give my men more assurance—you know."

There was plenty of room for an extra person. Even though the passenger capacity of the *Hindenburg* had been increased to 70 through the addition of 10 staterooms, there were only 36 on the manifest. The Redeerei took advantage by assigning an unusually large crew—61 officers and men instead of the usual 40—to engage in training.

The crew had plenty to do on Monday. The engines had to be tuned, gas pressure checked, navigation charts prepared, and passenger areas polished and dusted. Kubis and head chef Xavier Maier had to replace the food and wine "sampled" the previous day by SD troops. Two children were among the passengers, and stewardess Emilie Imhoff made sure there were toys and books on board. The last of the cargo was loaded and secured, including film, tobacco, merchandise for a Chicago store, airplane parts, two dogs, a woman's bathrobe, and three fertile partridge eggs.

INTERVIEW WITH THE SS

Meanwhile, in Berlin, more preparations were under way. Fritz Erdmann, Franz Witt, and Klaus Hinkelbein were scheduled to fly on the *Hindenburg* as ordinary passengers. In reality, they held the respective ranks of colonel, major, and lieutenant in the *Luftwaffe*, the German air force, and all were graduates of the *Luftwaffe*'s intelligence school.

The *Luftwaffe* routinely sent observers in civilian dress on overseas airship flights. It was not that Hermann Göring was interested in zeppelins as warships, but the trips gave his intelligence officers opportunities to get aerial views of ports and military installations in Britain, France, and the United States. What was not routine, however, was that the three officers had been ordered by the *Luftwaffe* to report to Berlin before the flight for a briefing by the SS.

At precisely 10 A.M., they were seated before the desk of Major Hufschmidt. The major got right to the point. He said that the zeppelins had become, as Goebbels had foreseen, a symbol of the increasing power of Hitler's Third Reich and of progress made under Nazi rule.

However, there were, he continued, subversive elements—Communists, Jews, labor agitators—who would stop at nothing to weaken Germany in the eyes of the world. One way would be to destroy the *Hindenburg*, a prominent symbol of Nazi might. Such an event could not be permitted, especially as it might happen in the United States with American lives lost. What Major Hufschmidt did not say, but everyone present understood, was that, should Germany eventually fight a European war, it wanted the United States to stay neutral.

The SS officer mentioned the letters of warning, particularly that of Kathie Rausch. Rausch, the SS had learned, was living with Georg Pfister, who had entered the United States illegally and worked as a cook at a Milwaukee hotel. Pfister had been supplying the SS with information on German communists in his city, so there was more reason to think Rausch's warning should be taken seriously.

"SUSPICIOUS" PASSENGERS

Hufschmidt then had an aide bring in a thick file. In it was information on each person who was to fly on the *Hindenburg*. Colonel Erdmann inquired as to why this was a *Luftwaffe* matter and not one for the gestapo or SS. Hufschmidt replied that, as a result of the previous year's controversy over the propaganda flight, ultimate responsibility for airship operations had been given to Göring and the *Luftwaffe*.

The first names on the list were, coincidently, the first that Hufschmidt said bore watching—Leonhard and Gertrude Adelt. Both were journalists, although Gertrud had recently had her press credentials removed for writing articles unflattering to the Nazis. Furthermore, they were close friends of

Stefan Zweig, a Jewish writer and prominent Hitler critic now living in London.

Six names from the top was that of Karl Clemens, a 26-year-old photographer on assignment from the Redeerei. This aroused suspicions because camera equipment could be used to set off a bomb. The trip had been arranged by company official Heinz Wronsky, recently expelled from the Nazi Party when his Jewish background was discovered. Also, Hufschmidt said, Eckener might have had a hand in the arrangements, and Eckener was still under suspicion.

Douglas Edwards was the next passenger to be singled out. A former U.S. Navy petty officer, he now worked in Germany for General Motors, which had numerous manufacturing plants there. Edwards, the SS major said, routinely collected information on German industries capable of producing military hardware and passed it along to the American Navy.

Moritz Feibusch was considered only a slight risk. The food importer from San Francisco had no known subversive connections, but he was Jewish—enough to raise suspicion in Nazi eyes.

Finally, Hufschmidt discussed Joseph Späh, a 35-year-old acrobat. He had been born in a part of Germany that, as a result of World War I, was now French. Späh thus carried a French passport although he and his family lived in the United States.

He had been observed, Hufschmidt said, living in a manner beyond his income and consorting with anti-Nazi elements. In addition, Späh had been frequently seen in the company of an exotic dancer named Mathia Merrifield, an American who was also close to an outspoken opponent of Hitler. Hufschmidt then concluded with vague remarks that the three *Luftwaffe* men should keep an eye on the passengers and take action to prevent sabotage.

As they rode to the airport to catch a flight for Frankfurt and the *Hindenburg*, the three officers reflected on what they had been told. Finally, Witt exclaimed, as quoted by Mooney,

The passenger cabins on the *Hindenburg* were located on the upper level, Deck A, and were similar to the sleeper cars that can be found on many trains. Remarkably, the lower level, Deck B, featured a smoking room for passengers. The room was specially designed to keep out hydrogen gas and prevent fires and explosions.

"Information derived from lovers of cooks, barmaids, whores, striptease dancers and acrobats is not what the *Luftwaffe* would rely on for accuracy."

THE INSPECTION

As the three officers headed for Frankfurt, their fellow passengers were gathering in that city's Frankfurter Hof hotel. Margaret Mather had flown from Cologne early that morning. Since she was already at the airport, she tried to have her luggage taken directly on board the *Hindenburg* only to be told that it would have to go to the hotel to be inspected with the rest. The inspection would not take place until afternoon, so she spent the day sightseeing.

At about 4 P.M., the passengers gathered in the hotel's main dining room. Some, like John Pannes and his wife, Emma, were veteran travelers. He managed the New York office of the Hamburg-American steamship company and had sailed with his wife to Germany specifically to make the first 1937 voyage of the *Hindenburg.* Others were not as experienced. Marie Kleeman, 61, had never flown before and was going to Massachusetts to visit her daughter.

Rudolph Anders, 65, a tea merchant from Dresden, Germany, and his son were going to New York on business. Two weeks prior to the flight, however, he canceled his son's reservation and sent him by ship, saying only, as quoted by Hoehling, "Can't have two from the same family on one airship." Having multiple family members on board did not bother Hermann Doehner, however. The drug company owner was taking his wife, Matilda; 16-year-old daughter, Irene; and his 8- and 6-year-old sons, Walter and Werner, back to their home in Mexico City.

The luggage inspection was far more thorough than usual, performed by SD officers as Redeerei employees stood by. Each piece was x-rayed, then opened. In some cases, inspectors slit suitcase linings to look inside. They opened every box, package, and bottle—sniffing shaving lotion and perfume. Clemens's photographic equipment underwent special scrutiny and his flashbulbs were confiscated. He protested that he would need them for interior shots, but to no avail.

The passengers had been given a list of items that would be removed from their luggage. Weapons were banned, but so were any items capable of causing a flame or an electric spark,

The Weight of Things

Keeping an airship's payload—crew, passengers, and cargo—as light as possible was always a concern. The more the total weight, the greater the volume of gas that had to be used for lift.

The design of the zeppelins and the rules for passengers and crew were designed to save as much weight as possible. All furniture was made of hollow aluminum sections and, according to Margaret Mather in *Harper's Monthly Magazine*, "were light as feathers and most comfortable." There was even a baby grand piano made mostly of aluminum, but it was not present on the *Hindenburg*'s final flight because the ship was scheduled to have 72 passengers on the return trip to Germany.

Crew members were allowed to take only minimal extra clothing and a few toiletries. Passengers were charged about one dollar per pound for anything over the 44-pound allowance. Mather's luggage was some 33 pounds overweight. The petite woman argued that she should not be charged extra since most of the male passengers outweighed her by far more than 33 pounds.

including not only flashbulbs but also batteries, lighters, and matches. Banned, too, were ways in which passengers could send unauthorized messages, including carrier pigeons.

AIRPORT ARRIVAL

It was not until about 7 P.M. that the passengers were loaded onto three buses and driven to the airport. Margaret Mather wrote in *Harper's* of seeing for the first time "the great silver ship, and at the sight a wave of joy swept over me." After one last inspection of tickets and passports, they were allowed to board.

One passenger was absent. Joseph Späh had somehow slipped away at the hotel and arrived on his own at the airport by taxi, a package under his arm. The package contained a doll, a last-minute purchase for a daughter back home. After the gift wrapping was undone and the doll minutely inspected, Späh was allowed on board.

Most of the passengers quickly deposited their hand luggage and other small items in their cabins and made their way to the windows to watch the liftoff. Despite the lateness of the hour, a sizable crowd was there to see the ship off; among the crowd was a detachment of Hitler Youth, in their uniform brown shirts with swastika armbands and black shorts. Much more colorful was a brass band decked out in blue and yellow.

The band first played "Muss I denn?," a sentimental ballad about parting from loved ones. Then came the "Horst Wessel" song, the Nazi anthem; and, finally, "Deutschland Über Alles," the German national anthem.

At last, about 8:15 P.M., the lines were cast off, and Knorr and Spehl disconnected the nose cone from the mooring mast. The band prepared to strike up one last song, but the ship drifted toward them, and they were forced to retreat. The bandleader raised his baton, but again the ship edged too close. Finally, after a third retreat, the band struck up

As the *Hindenburg* prepared to leave Germany, passengers stood at the airship's windows and watched the crowds that had gathered for the send-off. There was nothing particularly remarkable about the departure, although there had been concerns about the possibility of a bomb on board.

"A Mighty Fortress Is Our God," and the *Hindenburg* slowly began to rise. There was no sudden surge of movement, no roar of engines. The only way one passenger, college student Peter Belin, could tell the ship was moving was that the figures on the ground were growing smaller. "It was an indescribable feeling of lightness and buoyancy," Mather wrote, "a lift and pull upward, quite unlike the take off of an airplane."

When the ship reached an altitude of about 100 feet, the engines kicked in, and the giant propellers began to rotate with increasing speed. As the *Hindenburg* slowly picked up speed, the Hitler Youth broke ranks and scampered across the landing field, their caps falling off and their scarves flying in the breeze. They did not stop until they reached the fence surrounding the field. There, they stood, watching the *Hindenburg* as it slowly sailed out of sight—northwest toward the Rhine River, the ocean, and North America.

3 Journey

As the *Hindenburg* left Frankfurt behind, most passengers and crew settled in for a largely uneventful crossing. Some people, however, viewed others with suspicion, and perhaps one already knew how the journey would end.

The most direct course to the Atlantic Ocean would have been southwest over France, but the French, remembering World War I, would not allow it. They said that any German aircraft, even one carrying passengers, would be fired on if it attempted to cross French territory. England had not been as blunt, but still made it clear that the zeppelins were not welcome over the British Isles. The *Hindenburg*'s route, therefore, was up the Rhine, across Holland, through the English Channel past Dover, and out into the Atlantic.

Although night was falling and it had been a long day for all aboard, the passengers were mostly too excited to sleep. Many looked out the windows. Margaret Mather wrote in *Harper's Monthly Magazine* that the ship "passed hamlets and villages gleaming jewel-like in the darkness, and came to a great spreading mass of lights, which someone said was

Cologne, and suddenly we were looking down at the cathedral, beautifully clear and dark amid the glow."

A SNACK FOR ULLA

Since there had not been time for supper, chief steward Kubis and his assistants set out salad, cold meats, and biscuits at about 10 P.M. One passenger, however, needed special attention. Joseph Späh insisted on being taken to feed his dog Ulla. Kubis referred him to Captain Lehmann. Späh told Lehmann that the dog would be frightened and that he had been assured he would get to take care of her personally. Lehmann laughed and agreed.

The only way from the passenger section to the interior of the ship was through a door in Kubis's office. The steward led Späh through the door, past the crew's quarters to one of the gangways that ran the length of the ship. They walked back, almost to the end of the ship, to the animal hold, where Ulla got her meal. On the way back, Kubis emphasized to Späh that passengers were never allowed into the ship's interior on their own.

Shortly after midnight, the ship ran into a storm, one too large to steer around. Those passengers still awake looked nervously at the lightning flashes and jumped when thunder sounded, but they were assured by Kubis that they were completely safe. Indeed, the rain on the ship's skin had a soothing sound, and there was no motion or structural sounds as there would have been on an ocean liner. Thus comforted, the *Hindenburg* passengers spent their first night.

THE FIRST MORNING

They awoke on Tuesday to find the sky overcast and the ship still making its way into a strong wind. The airship was steady, however, and the passengers sat down to a hearty breakfast with no thought of motion sickness. With the gray sky above and a gray sea below, there was not much to look at, so they spent the rest of the morning in various ways.

George Grant retired to the smoking room to write in his diary. Gertrude Adelt and Margaret Mather spent most of the morning in their cabins, but the Doehner boys played on the floor of the lounge as their mother and sister watched. One of Werner's toys was a Mickey Mouse windup car that had to be confiscated by Kubis, who had noticed that it emitted sparks as it ran across the carpet.

Chief radio operator Willy Speck and his assistants were busy telegraphing dozens of messages—mostly greetings from the *Hindenburg*—sent by passengers to friends and relatives. If those sending the messages wanted to tell people exactly where they were, they could follow the ship's progress on a large map

The spacious dining room aboard the *Hindenburg* was just one of the many amenities available to the passengers. While dining on fine German cuisine served on gold and blue china, some of the passengers already were discussing plans for future trips on the *Hindenburg*.

next to the bust of President Hindenburg at the head of the stairs to B deck. Every few hours, a steward moved a little red flag to show the latest position.

Späh persuaded Kubis to take him for another visit to Ulla. He was surprised to see by the light coming through the ship's skin that the gangway he had traversed the previous night was so narrow and in some places lacked handrails. Kubis joked that moving around in the interior of the *Hindenburg* should be easy for an acrobat such as Späh.

LUXURIOUS LUNCH

Lunch was typically luxurious, featuring Rhine salmon à la Hindenburg and goose rolled in flour and fried in butter followed by pears covered with chocolate sauce. Moritz Feibusch

Luxury Travel

Hugo Eckener did everything he could to ensure that the *Graf Zeppelin* and *Hindenburg* provided as much comfort and as many luxuries as possible to their passengers. Margaret Mather, writing in *Harper's Monthly Magazine*, reported, "My bunk was narrow but most comfortable and furnished with fine linen sheets and soft light blankets. The walls of my tiny cabin were covered with pearl-gray linen. It was charming."

Later in the article, she described the lounge with its "great map of the world, painted in soft colors, showing the history of navigation, the routes and the ships of the first explorers, with their billowing sails and the modern liners, and above them all the beautiful, silver *Hindenburg* sailing the great circle."

was impressed with zeppelin travel. He told his tablemate, William Leuchtenburg, that he intended to bring his mother to the United States on the *Hindenburg* later that year. The elderly lady did not want to leave Germany, but conditions were rapidly worsening for Jews there. The Nazi Reichstag, or parliament, was passing laws to restrict Jews from entering business, and some park benches in Berlin carried signs saying *"Nicht für Juden"* ("not for Jews").

Kubis, meanwhile, fretted about unauthorized passengers gaining access to the ship's interior. Even though the only passenger entrance was through his office and all passengers were to be escorted, exceptions were possible. He was not on duty every minute, and one of his assistants might not be as vigilant. He knew, for instance, that chief engineer Sauter had allowed a passenger to take an unaccompanied tour.

On this Tuesday afternoon, however, the only tour was one authorized and led by the ship's doctor, Kurt Rüdiger, a young man only one year away from his studies. Späh was the first in the group to don the required canvas shoes. Other members included Irene Doehner, Peter Belin, and Leonhard and Gertrude Adelt.

When the group passed the animal hold, Späh announced that he wanted to visit his dog. When Rüdiger said that the group was supposed to stay together, Späh invited everyone to come say hello to Ulla. When Rüdiger protested that there was no time, Späh airily told him to take the group ahead and that he would catch up. Rüdiger reluctantly did so, and Späh was left alone at ring No. 62 between gas cells Nos. 4 and 5. He rejoined them later, and the group finished the tour, after which Rüdiger reported Späh's rule violation.

Supper consisted of pâté, small fillets of roast beef, salad, cheese, and fruit. Unlike the previous evening, there was little excitement and little to do. Most of the passengers went to bed early. Even the aluminum piano was absent, eliminated to save weight on what was to be a sold-out return voyage.

WEDNESDAY MORNING

At 6 A.M. on Wednesday, the *Hindenburg* was about 620 miles east of St. John's, Newfoundland, more than halfway across the Atlantic. Headwinds were still high—about 50 miles per hour—and the ship was some 10 hours behind schedule. The weather ahead did not look favorable, either. These storms were predicted to be in the Lakehurst area around the time the ship was to land.

At midmorning, Späh decided to get some exercise and wanted to take a longer walk than was possible in the passenger section. He went to Kubis's office, found it empty, and decided to go into the interior on his own. He walked back to visit his dog in the stern, climbed the ladder to the upper gangway, walked all the way to the bow, then descended the ladder and went back to his starting point—about 600 yards in all.

He was on his second time around when he ran into Helmut Lau. The SS sergeant led him firmly back to Kubis's office. The chief steward had returned and told Späh he would have to report this second violation to Captain Pruss.

Pruss, meanwhile, had ordered a complete inspection of the ship, something out of the ordinary during the course of a voyage. Chief rigger Knorr, assisted by Erich Spehl, had the job of examining the gas cells. Knorr would start near the front at No. 16, Spehl would go to the stern and start at No. 1, and they would meet in the middle between Nos. 8 and 9. It was a tedious job that involved climbing the flues between each bag, testing the bags for pressure, looking for tears, examining cords and netting. After about six hours of work, Knorr had found nothing amiss. Spehl told him that all was well with the rear cells, as well.

AN ODD QUESTION

By the time the inspection was finished, it was midafternoon on board and about 7 P.M. in Frankfurt. Spehl's girlfriend showed up at the Redeerei offices. As on a prior visit, she

Landing the *Hindenburg* involved anchoring the dirigible to prevent it from floating away. As shown in this photo of a previous landing, the craft's crew dropped ropes during its descent, and men on the ground grabbed on and guided the ship to its resting spot.

asked if there was any news of the *Hindenburg*. The clerks, unaware that the flight was hours behind schedule, told her once again that the ship would land on time at 6 A.M. New Jersey time.

The Redeerei clerks were not the only ones who thought the flight was proceeding as planned. In New York City, police detective Arthur Johnson packed a small overnight bag. He would drive to Lakehurst to spend the night prior to what he thought would be the 6 A.M. landing of the *Hindenburg*.

In Chicago, Herb Morrison, a week away from his 32nd birthday, packed not only a suitcase but also his broadcasting equipment for the flight he and his engineer, Charles Nehlsen, would take to New Jersey. Their assignment was to meet the *Hindenburg*, describe the landing, and record interviews with some of the passengers. The description and interviews would not be broadcast live but would be recorded for playback that Saturday on station WLS's *Dinner Bell* show.

LONG WAITS

Those expecting the *Hindenburg* on Thursday morning, however, were in for a long wait. The Redeerei and the U.S. Navy had long ago decided that landings at Lakehurst would be at either 6 A.M. or 6 P.M., the most convenient hours for Commander Rosendahl to muster his ground crew of sailors and local civilians. The adverse winds, however, had made a 6 A.M. landing impossible. On Wednesday afternoon, Captain Pruss sent a message to Lakehurst that the landing would have to wait until 6 P.M.

Meanwhile, the *Hindenburg* was flying in sunshine for the first time since liftoff, and the mood of the passengers brightened accordingly. Newfoundland came into view, signaling the beginning of the end of the journey. "We glimpsed the foothills, the lighthouse on Cape Race, the limitless forests of the hinterland," Leonhard Adelt wrote in *Reader's Digest*. "Then the coast sprang back and we again floated, a gray object in gray mist, over the invisible sea."

Some people, however, had little time for or interest in the sights below. A radio broadcast from Berlin had carried the story of the sabotage of a French train. The news bothered Colonel Erdmann, who remembered his instructions from the SS. After learning from Major Witt about Joseph Späh's unauthorized trips into the interior, Erdmann decided to take action.

The two officers, along with Lieutenant Hinkelbein, went to see Captain Lehmann. Erdmann suggested that, with only a little over 24 hours remaining in the voyage, Späh be confined to his cabin as a precaution.

The *Luftwaffe* officers presented a strong case, but Lehmann had doubts. Part of his mission was to seek a partner-

The View

Cloudy, rainy weather prevented the *Hindenburg* passengers from having much of a view on the first two days of their voyage. On the morning before landing, however, the sun shined as Newfoundland came into sight. Leonhard Adelt described the passengers' excitement in a *Reader's Digest* article:

> Binoculars and cameras appeared, and my wife's delight grew when the white dots along the coast turned out to be icebergs. The captain ordered the ship to fly low and steer toward them. Very slowly we passed over the most beautiful, which looked like a magic marble statue. The sun came out and laid a double rainbow around the airship. The giant iceberg turned into a monument of sparkling brilliants [diamonds].

ship in the United States, he said, and arresting an American resident—even one traveling on a French passport—would be troublesome, especially on such slim evidence. Lehmann urged Erdmann not to press his case and told the officers to try to enjoy their last night on the *Hindenburg* and that he would try to do his part by furnishing music.

Lehmann was as good as his word. There was no piano, but after dinner he played his accordion for hours in the lounge— folk songs, show tunes, waltzes—with the passengers singing along. So, it was in a merry mood that most of the passengers retired for the evening. Margaret Mather wrote in *Harper's* that "I slept like a child and awoke in the morning with a feeling of well being and happiness such as one rarely experiences after youth has passed."

Not everyone slept as well. During the party, as Lehmann played his accordion, steward Eugen Nunnenmacher accidentally stained his white jacket. He ran to his cabin to get another, only to find a roommate, Erich Spehl, groaning and thrashing in his sleep. Nunnenmacher shook him awake, asking what was wrong. The groggy Spehl could not answer, and Nunnenmacher returned to his duties.

THURSDAY MORNING

When the sun rose shortly before 6 A.M. on Thursday, May 6, the *Hindenburg* was off the North American coast about 350 miles from Boston. More rain was forecast for the New Jersey area. Lakehurst radioed that it would collect weather information at 1:30 P.M. and relay it to the airship along with probable landing conditions.

Many of the passengers who had stayed up late listening to and singing along with Captain Lehmann slept late as well—including Margaret Mather. She ate breakfast, packed her luggage and suddenly, as she wrote in *Harper's*, "we were flying over Boston."

Captain Pruss wanted to give his passengers a chance to see Boston, and he wanted to give Boston a chance to see the *Hindenburg.* He brought the airship down to where it broke through the cloud cover only a few feet above the Customs House tower. In the harbor, ships blew their steam whistles in salute. Automobiles pulled off to the sides of streets, and drivers emerged to gaze upward.

The ship caused quite a commotion in the countryside as well. Mather wrote, "Our passing frightened the dogs, who rushed to their houses, and caused a great commotion in the barnyards—especially among the chickens and pigs; the latter rushed desperately to and fro, and seemed absolutely terrified, and the chickens fluttered and ran about in proverbial fashion. Cows and sheep did not notice us much."

DELAYED LANDING

At Lakehurst, Rosendahl and his staff were starting their preparations for the landing. The weather forecast was not good, but there was a chance the predicted rainstorms would moderate in time. Lieutenant Raymond Tyler, the naval officer who would be in command of the landing party, spent much of the morning reviewing procedures. An abnormally extensive review was necessary because a "high" landing was scheduled rather than the more usual "low" landing.

A low landing called for the captain to bring the ship in slowly just above ground level, much like an airplane landing, coming to a gentle stop near the mast. It would then be the job of the ground crew hauling on ropes to pull the ship into place. With a high landing, the ship was eased to a stop at the top of the mast, connected to the mast by wires, then pulled down by the ground crew until a cone on the very tip of the ship's bow was able to fit into a socket receptacle at the bottom. The Redeerei was trying to change from low to high landings because the latter involved a smaller ground crew and thus saved money.

As the day wore on, reporters assigned to cover the landing began to gather. Since it was the *Hindenburg*'s first voyage of the season, a fairly large number of newspapers and magazines were represented, although not nearly so many as during the inaugural season the previous year. Joining the reporters were friends and relatives of the passengers. Some had been on hand since dawn, having not received word of the delay. Joseph Späh's wife and three children were there, as were Peter Belin's parents, Leonhard Adelt's brother, and Margaret Mather's sister-in-law and niece. Others were there simply out of curiosity.

The *Hindenburg*'s crew, like the men on the ground, were making preparations for landing. All hands were busy, not only those involved in the landing operation itself. Kubis and his assistants served lunch early so that Maier and the kitchen staff could stow their gear. The stewards then went around to each cabin, gathering sheets and pillowcases to be laundered. Packed luggage was stacked under the statue of President Hindenburg on the A deck to be ready for unloading.

OVER NEW YORK CITY

But there was more sightseeing aside for the passengers as Pruss guided the ship into New York harbor and over Manhattan Island. Leonhard Adelt wrote in *Reader's Digest* that the skyscrapers looked like "a board full of nails." He could see the observation deck of the Empire State Building crowded with photographers.

The ship also flew over Brooklyn, only 600 feet above the Ebbets Field baseball diamond, where there was a game in progress. The fans stopped watching the game to gaze upward at the *Hindenburg*. The Brooklyn Dodger and Pittsburgh Pirate players did not mind. They were watching the ship, too.

At 4 P.M., Captain Albert Sammt was relieved as watch officer. Sammt conducted his usual brief inspection of the ship, walking the interior gangway from bow to stern, casting his experienced eye over rings, girders, and wiring. He checked the rope netting holding the gas cells in place, visually checked the cells themselves, and returned to the control gondola to report that all was well.

A few minutes before Sammt was relieved, Lakehurst had radioed the *Hindenburg* that winds at ground level were blowing at 25 knots, or about 29 miles per hour—too strong for a landing attempt. Pruss guided the ship over the landing field and dropped a message tied to a weight. It read, "Riding out the storm."

At about 5 P.M., the storm seemed to be lessening, and Commander Rosendahl decided it was time to summon the ground crew. At the sound of the air station's steam whistle, U.S. Navy sailors assigned to landing duty emerged from their barracks. In the neighboring town of Lakehurst, civilians hired to help left their homes and walked or rode bicycles to the landing site. One man, Allen Hagaman, had not had time to finish his supper. He grabbed a ham sandwich and walked down the street, watched from the window by his daughter Sarah, who would soon go on her own to watch the ship come in.

At 5:12, Lakehurst advised the *Hindenburg* that a rain shower was moving over the field from the west but that the wind had dropped to 18 miles per hour. Pruss replied, asking about visibility. Lakehurst said that visibility was only about eight miles and recommended additional delay. Pruss agreed.

Word of the *Hindenburg*'s status had been telephoned to New York City's Biltmore Hotel, where the passengers booked on the return trip were assembled for the scheduled midnight liftoff. Company officials checked their passports and tickets and weighed their luggage. There was not even a cursory inspection of the luggage as opposed to what had taken place in Germany.

KNORR'S INSPECTION

At 6 P.M., chief rigger Knorr relieved Erich Spehl. Like Captain Sammt, Knorr had a habit when going off duty of making

Because the *Hindenburg* was making its first transatlantic flight of the season, the event drew a large crowd of press and spectators *(above)*. As the airship approached, cameras captured the moment and journalists began to broadcast their descriptions of the dirigible and its descent over the radio.

an inspection, part of which was to push his hand against each gas cell. There were gauges by which pressure could be read, of course, but an old airship man like Knorr could sense by feel if something was wrong.

Something was wrong now. The pressure of cell No. 4 felt low. Knorr feared there was a tear somewhere in the fabric. After landing, he and his assistants would have to find the tear—possibly a lengthy search—and mend it. On his way back to the crew quarters, he mentioned his concern to Kubis, who mentally began to prepare for a departure of 3 A.M. or even later.

At 6:44 P.M., shortly after receiving Rosendahl's recommendation that he land, Pruss sent word that he was setting his course for a final approach to Lakehurst. At 7 P.M., he gave the command "landing stations" to the crew. Chief engineer Sauter was stationed at the stern just above the bottom vertical fin. With him were Lau, Hans Freund, and Richard Kollmer. Freund and Lau were assigned to drop the stern yaw lines, the ones that would keep the ship from drifting side-to-side. Kollmer would lower the main stern mooring cable and also man the small landing wheel on the bottom of the fin.

Their counterparts in the bow—Ludwig Felber, Alfred Bernhard, and Erich Spehl—were supervised by Knorr. The three men would handle the nose cone connection and the main line by which the ship would be winched from the top of the mast to the bottom.

By this time, the ground crew had been assembled on the landing field. As the ship descended along the mast, it was to be guided into place—and eventually held down—by 119 men on the landing lines—68 at the bow and 46 at the stern. Crew members on the ship would drop steel cables called "spiders" along which were multiple manila ropes, each with a wooden handle. It was the line handlers' job to bring the ship down to the proper point and then manually hold it down—fighting crosswinds if necessary—while another 80 men secured the ship to two heavy railroad cars at the bow and stern. The cars were on circular tracks so that, in case of an abnormally strong wind, the ship could move around like a weather vane, pointing into the wind.

FIRST LINES DROPPED

The landing lines were dropped at 7:21 P.M. The bow lines uncoiled without any trouble, snaked through a small hatch on the underside of the ship, and fell to the ground. One of the stern lines, however, became caught momentarily in a bracing wire near its hatch at ring No. 47. Freund and Lau climbed up a flight of stairs to clear it. A few feet above their heads were gas cells No. 4 and 5.

Once the line was clear, it fell to the ground like the rest. As each hit the earth, onlookers could see clouds of dust puff up, a fact that would later become important.

The *Hindenburg* was now only about 150 feet off the ground, the line handlers straining to keep it steady. One of the officers supervising the mast crew, Lieutenant R.W. Antrim, quoted in Hoehling's *Who Destroyed the Hindenburg?*, saw a portion of the skin behind one of the engine gondolas become "very loose and fluttering." Reporter Alice Hager, also quoted by Hoehling, saw a "rippling."

As the ship drifted lower, line handler Francis Hyland was looking up toward the lower fin, hoping to see the large signature he had placed there the previous year. To his surprise, he saw what appeared to be backfire coming out of the rear engine on the port, or left, side of the aircraft. Another observer, W.W. Groves, an engineer who had come to check the ship's copper tubing, is quoted by Hoehling as having seen a spark "like static electricity" underneath the ship not far from the stern.

It was now 7:25 P.M. Freund and Lau had just finished clearing the jammed landing line when Lau, who happened to be looking up at gas cell No. 4, saw a bright flash and a noise that he later compared to a gas stove being ignited. Freund and Sauter heard it, too, and looked up in time to see a yellow-orange glow about three feet across inside the cell. Of all the calamities that could befall a hydrogen-filled airship, this was the one most feared and against which the most stringent precautions had been taken. The *Hindenburg* was on fire!

4 Inferno

From the time when Helmut Lau, Hans Freund, and Rudolf Sauter first saw a glow inside gas cell No. 4, it was a matter of only a few seconds until the *Hindenburg* was a flaming inferno sinking slowly toward the earth. For the spectators, it was a scene of horror. For the passengers and crew, it was "a living hell," as described by Freund in Hoehling's *Who Destroyed the Hindenburg?*

Sauter had the sudden impression of a *blitzlicht*, or flash-bulb, going off. Richard Kollmer, who had been looking down instead of up, said in a *New York Times* article that the sound was "like a rifle shot."

As the four men watched, unable to move, the glow grew larger and brighter. Then, as Lau said in the *New York Times*, "the cell suddenly disappeared under the heat" with a tremendous whooshing sound. In Hoehling's book, Lau said he recalled seeing "aluminum parts and fabric parts thrown up" into the air then start to fall toward the crewmen. Kollmer recalled in the *New York Times* article being "suddenly surrounded by fire."

Sauter shouted for everyone to get down and stay down. Lau dived for the floor at the bottom of the ship where the fin was attached. Freund landed on top of him, and Kollmer and Sauter followed. They huddled there, hands over their heads, as burning fiber and red-hot aluminum showered down around them.

GLOW ON THE GROUND

The people on the ground soon became aware of the disaster. The rear part of the ship seemed to glow, one witness comparing the sight to a Japanese lantern and another, according to

What began as a small spark became an inferno as the *Hindenburg*'s hydrogen cells caught fire. The ground crew fled when hot pieces of the great dirigible showered the area. Passengers, slow to realize the situation, began to leap from the main lounge of the ship. It was during this horrifying chaos that journalist Herb Morrison uttered the famous words, "Oh the humanity!"

Hoehling, reporting "a faint pink glow in the lower center of the ship . . . like some thick silvery fish with a rosy glow in the abdomen."

Then, as gas cell No. 4 incinerated, a small plume of flame erupted outside the ship just in front of the top fin. Commander Rosendahl saw the flame and said later, as quoted in the *New York Times*, that he knew "it spelled doom" for the ship. Other witnesses mentioned seeing the flame, and one mentioned a shower of sparks, as well.

In the next instant, the entire rear of the *Hindenburg* was a mass of flames. Fed by a sudden supply of oxygen, the hydrogen cells burned with a bright, yellow-white heat. One of the reporters present, Henry W. Roberts of the *Aero Digest*, later wrote, as quoted by Michael Mooney in *The Hindenburg*, that the fire was as bright as "a thousand, ten thousand magnesium flares," casting a brilliant light on what had a few moments before been Lakehurst at sunset. William Craig, a Standard Oil Company employee at Lakehurst, told the *New York Times* that the men gathered immediately underneath the ship—landing crew, photographers, and reporters—"once the horrible shock had passed and they raced madly in all directions to escape the flaming, falling ship."

MORRISON'S MOMENT

It was at this moment that Herb Morrison earned his place in broadcasting history. The Chicago announcer had just finished a description of the fading sunlight's reflection off the *Hindenburg*'s windows when the flames erupted. Morrison then exclaimed, as quoted on the Internet site Electricinca,

> It's burst into flames! Get out of the way, get out of the way. Get this, Charlie, get this, Charlie. This fire . . . and it's crashing, it's crashing terrible. Oh, my, get out of the way please, it's burning, bursting into flames and it's falling on

the mooring mast and all the folks agree that this is terrible, this is the worst of the worst catastrophes in the world.

A sudden lurch was the first indication to the control gondola crew that something was wrong. Anton Witteman asked Pruss if a rope was broken. According to Hoehling, Pruss answered simply, "No." It was only when they saw a red glow on the ground beneath them that they realized what had happened. Everyone remained calm except helmsman Kurt Schönherr, who began moaning in terror. There was nothing left for them to do except to ride the *Hindenburg* down and jump from a window when the ground was close enough.

Phoning It In

The scheduled landing of the *Hindenburg* at the Lakehurst Naval Air Station was news, but not big news—at least not as big as its inaugural flight to the United States the previous year. Even so, newspapers, magazines, and newsreel companies sent crews to cover this first landing of 1936.

One lazy and eventually very unlucky reporter for the International News Service decided he did not need to go to Lakehurst. Equipped beforehand with the passenger list, he spent the afternoon in a bar, phoning in his story at the appropriate time he thought the *Hindenburg* would land.

When he discovered what had happened, he did not even bother to go back to his office, knowing he would be fired. He was, and so was a newsreel cameraman who grew bored with waiting, left the field during the afternoon, and went to a movie and lost track of the time.

THE PASSENGERS' REACTIONS

The passengers also were slow to realize their peril. Leonhard Adelt wrote in *Reader's Digest* that soon after he heard the noise that reminded him of a bottle being opened, he looked out the window to see "a delicate rose glow, as though the Sun was about to rise." Otto Clemens, taking pictures through a window, had no idea that the brightness he saw on the ground was reflected flame and that his photographs showed members of the landing crew already running.

The ship lurched, slanting abruptly back toward the stern as the exploding cells robbed the rear section of its buoyancy. The passengers in the lounge tumbled over one another, ending up against the rear wall in a tangle of arms, legs, and furniture. Margaret Mather wrote later in *Harper's* that she found herself pinned under several people and thought she might be suffocated, but she was suddenly free, just in time to see "long tongues of flame, bright red and very beautiful."

She saw her fellow passengers "leaping up and down amid the flames . . . it was like a scene from a medieval picture of hell." Many were bloody from having banged against furniture. One man cried out, she wrote, *"Es ist das Ende"*—"It is the end."

THE BYSTANDERS REACT

Certainly many of those watching thought that the end had come for the relatives they had come to welcome. Joseph Späh's wife, Vera, was praying. She had been to Roman Catholic Mass that morning and still had her rosary beads. Her four-year-old son, Gillie, Mooney wrote, kept saying, "Please don't let my Daddy die." Peter Belin's parents watched, horrified, from their car, certain that their son would be killed.

Belin and Späh, in fact, were preparing to jump, Späh having used a movie camera to smash through a window. The two men, plus another, climbed through the opening and hung onto a railing, waiting for the ship to fall to a safer level. The other man could not hold on. He lost his grip on the rail and grabbed the lapel of Späh's coat in desperation. The material ripped and Späh and Belin watched their unfortunate companion fall about 100 feet, hit the ground, and lie still. The remaining two waited and finally jumped at a height Späh later estimated to be about 40 feet. Both survived.

Some, however, did not. Craig said in the *New York Times* that he saw "at least a dozen people jumping from the forward end of the ship. Some were in flames as they plunged to earth."

Clemens was also preparing to jump. Beside him was John Pannes. Clemens told the *New York Times* that he said, "Come on, Mr. Pannes, jump." His fellow passenger replied, "Wait until I get my wife" and ran back toward the flaming cabin section.

MARGARET MATHER'S ESCAPE

Margaret Mather, meanwhile, was holding her coat up around her face, trying to protect it from the fire. She had seen people jumping out at what she assumed was a suicidal height. Suddenly, she later wrote, "I heard a loud cry! 'Come out, lady!' I looked, and we were on the ground. Two or three men were peering in, beckoning and calling to us." Instinctively, she searched for her purse before realizing how foolish that was. The men at the window called out again, and she climbed out to safety.

Matilda Doehner was frantically trying to get her children through those same windows. She had screamed for her husband, Hermann, when the fire had reached the passenger compartment, but could not see him anywhere. As the ship fell toward the ground, she told the *New York Times*, "I realized that the only hope of saving my children was to throw them clear."

She first tried to throw her daughter, Irene, through a window just before the ship crashed, but the 16-year-old was too heavy. She did manage, however, to pick up six-year-old Werner and toss him to members of the ground crew below. Then, she helped Irene and eight-year-old Walter, whose hair was on fire, to climb through and jump before jumping out herself.

One of the crew members, steward Eugen Nunnenmacher, caught Irene. Her clothes were ablaze, and she was badly burned in several places. Captain Bauer appeared, and the two men dragged the girl away from the ship by her arms, but some of her charred flesh came off in their hands.

Nunnenmacher returned to the ship to see if he could do any more. As he did so, he saw a strange sight. The mechanism holding one of the passenger gangways in place had given way, and the foot of the staircase had descended to the ground. Marie Kleeman, the 61-year-old woman on her first air voyage,

Through a Sea of Fire

As the bottom of the stricken *Hindenburg* sank lower, many passengers jumped from dining room or lounge windows. Leonhard Adelt wrote in *Reader's Digest* about the unreality of the situation:

> Reality ceased with one stroke as though fate in its cruelty was yet compassionate enough to withdraw from its victims the consciousness of their horror. I do not know, and my wife does not know, how we leaped from the airship. . . . We collapsed on our knees, and the impenetrable darkness of black clouds, shot through with flames, enveloped us. . . . We bent the hot metal with our bare hands without feeling pain. We freed ourselves and ran through a sea of fire. It was like a dream. Our bodies had no weight. They floated like stars through space.

came down the stairs just as she would have after a normal landing. Archbold's book quotes Rosendahl as saying Mrs. Kleeman looked as if she were "walking in her sleep." Behind her came Otto and Else Ernst. Otto Ernst was badly burned, and Nunnenmacher had to help him down.

ESCAPE FROM THE STERN

The stern of the *Hindenburg* had made contact with the ground first. Almost miraculously, the four men who had been closest to the initial explosion were still alive and relatively unharmed, huddled at the base of the lower fin. When he realized the stern was on the ground, Kollmer tried to open the hatch leading outside from the fin, but it was jammed shut. He then tore a hole in the outer skin and climbed out. Lau and Freund followed, with Sauter coming last, blood streaming from a head cut.

The four men ran to escape the wreck. As Sauter ran, however, he began to hear screams from passengers and his crewmates still trying to escape. He turned back, intending to join the rescue effort, but Navy sailors restrained him and took him to a nearby hangar for first aid.

The Navy men were, in fact, performing repeated acts of heroism. With the help of some of the local civilians, they began running up to the windows of the passenger deck and control gondola, even climbing inside on occasion to pull survivors to safety. Gill Wilson, aviation director for the state of New Jersey, told the *New York Times*, "Those boys dived into the flames like dogs after rabbits."

One of the men ran from the falling *Hindenburg* with a purpose in mind other than escape. Police detective Arthur Johnson was under the ship when it caught fire. His first thought was to get to a telephone, and he began running toward a hangar where he knew a pay phone was located. Overweight and not in good physical condition, he fell repeatedly before finally reaching the hangar. He pulled out one of the nickels

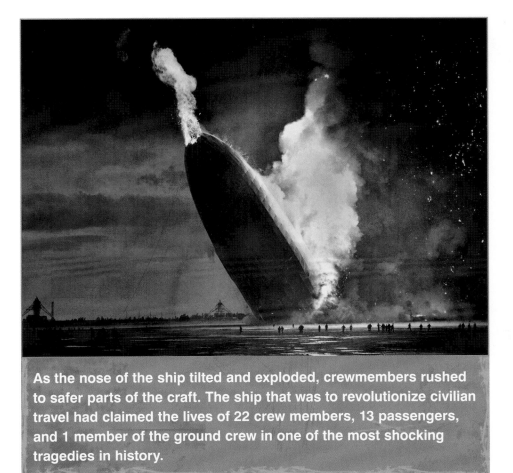

As the nose of the ship tilted and exploded, crewmembers rushed to safer parts of the craft. The ship that was to revolutionize civilian travel had claimed the lives of 22 crew members, 13 passengers, and 1 member of the ground crew in one of the most shocking tragedies in history.

he always carried for such emergencies and placed the call pleading for police, medical personnel, and ambulances.

OTHER CALLS

There were other frantic telephone calls to be made. An American Airlines plane was on hand to take some of the passengers on a short flight to Newark, New Jersey. Even as the pilot, in a hangar at the time of the crash, became certain there would be no survivors, a man stumbled in looking for a telephone. The person was passenger Herbert O'Laughlin. "His face was black, but he seemed to be all right," the pilot told the *New York Times*, "He wanted to telephone his mother in Chicago."

Numerous members of the landing party would suffer injuries, few of them serious. There was only one fatality among them. Allen Hagaman had been immediately under the control gondola when it crashed to Earth. When his body was recovered, an uneaten ham sandwich was found in his coat pocket.

Many of those fleeing from the wreck took time to look back on the scene. What they saw was a blazing fire rapidly devouring the *Hindenburg* from the stern forward. It had now moved well to the front of the control gondola. Hoehling's book quotes Rosendahl as recalling seeing the fire "greedily devouring the illustrious name 'HINDENBURG' letter by letter."

When Kollmer turned to look at the ship, it seemed to crack in the middle, the bow tilting up at a steep angle. Flames began to shoot from the nose. He wondered if any of his crewmates were trapped there.

DEATH IN THE BOW

Indeed, they were. Six men had been assigned to the nose of the ship to help secure it to the landing mast. Pruss had sent six more men there in an effort to balance the ship. Now, with the *Hindenburg* at a steep angle, the 12 men hung onto whatever was in reach, looking down along the interior of the ship as cell after cell erupted in flame.

As the fire grew closer, the girders to which the men clung grew hotter. Finally, some of them could hold on no longer. Erich Spehl was the first to let go, plunging down into the advancing fire. Seven others followed, including chief rigger Ludwig Knorr. Electrician Josef Leibrecht, cook Alfred Grözinger, and navigator Kurt Bauer managed to hold on, ignoring the burning of their hands and arms, until the bow crashed to Earth. Only then did they release their hold and run through the fire to safety.

At about this time, Herb Morrison was continuing to record his broadcast:

> It's a terrific blaze ladies and gentlemen. The smoke and the flames now and the frame is crashing to the ground. Not quite to the mooring masts. Oh the humanity, and all the passengers screaming around it. . . . Oh. I can't talk, ladies and gentlemen, honest it's just laying there, a mass of smoking wreckage. . . . Listen folks, I'm going to have

Passengers and crew members trapped aboard the *Hindenburg* attempted to escape in whatever way they could. Some lucky people were able to run off the ship as its aluminum frame slammed into the ground *(above, lower right hand corner)*. One surviving passenger, Werner Doehner, remembers being thrown out a dining room window by his mother after she had tossed his brother out of the same opening. She later followed, but failed to save Doehner's sister or father.

to stop for a minute because I'm lost for words. This is the worst thing I've ever witnessed.

THE CONTROL GONDOLA

Certainly it was a nightmare come true for the men in the control gondola, many of whom had flown hundreds of thousands of miles without any kind of accident. Witteman later recounted, as told in the *New York Times*, that he was "standing behind Captain Lehmann and saw him, Captain Pruss and Captain Sammt step out of a window." As he was about to follow them, Witteman saw "a great sheet of flame extending from the ship to the ground overtake them." He retreated and found another exit.

As Lehmann stumbled away from the ship, he was met by Rosendahl and Lieutenant George Watson, the Lakehurst public relations officer, running toward the control gondola. According to Hoehling, the German captain was muttering repeatedly, *"Das versteh ich nicht"*—"I don't understand." At first he did not appear to be seriously hurt, but when he walked past Watson, the young officer turned and saw that Lehmann's back was a mass of burns. Rosendahl then led his old friend away.

Sammt, meanwhile, had run—eyes closed against a thick pall of smoke—through a hail of burning debris and falling metal after jumping out a window. His uniform caught fire, and he rolled around in the still-damp grass and sand until the flames were out. He stood and cautiously opened his eyes, assuring himself he could still see. What met his gaze was Pruss walking toward him, hatless and with his hair completely burned off.

There were other stories of escape from the burning ship, but few could match that of Werner Franz, the *Hindenburg*'s 14-year-old cabin boy. He was in the officers' dining room when the first explosions took place and was thrown to the floor. He got to his feet, ran to a gangway, and was able to jump through a window.

Even though he was outside the ship, however, he was completely surrounded by red-hot girders and wires; flaming materials from the ship's skin; and thick, black smoke. But just when it seemed that he would be killed, a water tank burst above his head. He and the burning material around him were drenched in hundreds of gallons of water. The deluge also cleared the smoke enough for Franz to run to safety, unharmed.

A FLAMING WRECK

Finally, the stricken *Hindenburg* lay on the ground about 700 feet from the mooring mast. The millions of cubic feet of hydrogen had disappeared in a yellow-white blaze, but the diesel fuel still burned with a red glow and sent black smoke billowing into the increasing darkness. The twisted Duralumin girders still glowed. It would be many hours before anyone could approach the wreckage, let alone search it.

Most of the passengers and crew had escaped. Some were miraculously unhurt. Others were injured, some so seriously that they would not survive. Still others remained in the wreckage, their bodies yet to be found and identified.

In days to come, as part of the investigation of the disaster, newsreel cameramen would study their film. By measuring the length of film from the first frame showing the ship on fire to the final frame of the ship burning on the ground, and knowing the speed of the film as it went through their cameras, they could calculate exactly the elapsed time. The entire incident, which had seen the mighty *Hindenburg* transformed from airborne marvel to smoldering, twisted skeleton, had lasted 32 seconds.

5 Aftermath

The hours and days following the destruction of the *Hindenburg* brought suffering and death to the Lakehurst area and shock and disbelief to Germany. But, even as the injured were treated and the dead mourned, people and governments on both sides of the Atlantic vowed to keep the airship movement alive. The psychological impact of the disaster on the public and the hydrogen-helium question, however, presented serious barriers to the future.

The survivors' condition was, of course, the most immediate concern. Ambulances and medical personnel had responded to Detective Johnson's telephone call. As the injured ran from or were pulled from the burning ship, they were taken to a hangar where a makeshift emergency room had been set up.

When Margaret Mather arrived and was seated, a mild solution of prussic acid was applied to the burns on her hands. Captain Lehmann sat on a table nearby. His hair and much of his clothing had been burned off.

"Now his face was grave and calm," Mather wrote in *Harper's* of the usually jolly Lehmann. "And not a groan escaped his lips. His mental anguish must have been as intense as his physical pains, but he gave no sign of either. . . ."

Finally, an ambulance was available to take Mather to her niece's house in nearby Princeton, New Jersey. Her niece and sister-in-law had already returned from Lakehurst, certain that Mather had been killed. When they recovered from the shock of seeing her alive on their front porch, they called her brother in New York City.

LEHMANN'S LAST MOMENTS

Lehmann, meanwhile, was transferred to a nearby hospital. "I intended to stay with the ship as long as I could—until we could land her, if possible, but it was impossible" the *New York Times* reported him as saying. "Everything around me was on fire."

Lehmann died shortly after 5 P.M. on Friday, the day after the disaster. Early that morning, Rosendahl visited his bedside. Lehmann repeated what he had said immediately after the airship crashed—that he could not understand what had happened. Rosendahl later reported to the Federal Bureau of Investigation that Lehmann suspected sabotage.

At another hospital nearby, Matilda Doehner was treated for burns. She then kept watch over her younger son, Werner, who was not expected to live. Her husband had not been found, and it was assumed his body was one of those yet to be identified. When she asked about Irene, she was told that her daughter's condition was such that she could not be seen. Actually, the 16-year-old had already died, but doctors feared the news would be too much of a shock. Only after Werner improved was Matilda told of her daughter's death.

THE DEATH TOLL

Altogether, 35 of the 97 people aboard the *Hindenburg* either were killed in the fire and crash or else died later of their injuries. Thirteen passengers lost their lives, including Hermann and Irene Doehner, Colonel Erdman, John and Emma Pannes, and Moritz Feibusch.

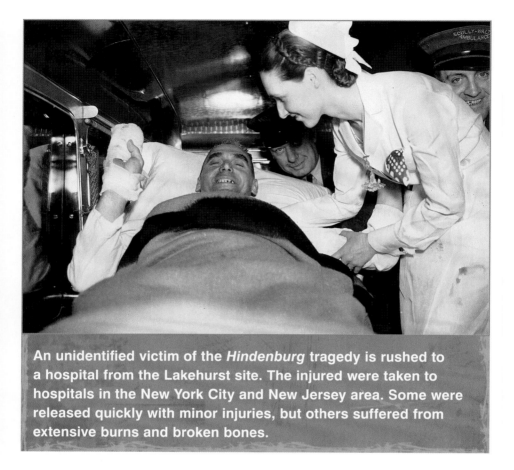

An unidentified victim of the *Hindenburg* tragedy is rushed to a hospital from the Lakehurst site. The injured were taken to hospitals in the New York City and New Jersey area. Some were released quickly with minor injuries, but others suffered from extensive burns and broken bones.

Twenty-two crew members perished. The greatest loss of life was among the dozen men who had been in the ship's bow, but other fatalities included chief radio operator Willy Speck and Emilie Imhoff, the world's first—and as it turned out, last—zeppelin stewardess. The last person to die was passenger Otto Ernst, who succumbed to his burns nine days after the fire. Of the hundreds of people on the ground, the only fatality was that of Alan Hagaman.

Of the living, 30 remained in hospitals throughout the New Jersey–New York City area. One of these was Captain Pruss. At first, he was given little chance to live, but he rallied with the aid of blood transfusions and on May 24 was declared out of danger.

In a statement printed by the *New York Times*, he expressed thanks for the "countless demonstrations of friendship and gratitude" shown to the *Hindenburg* crew by the American people.

Some of the survivors were uninjured or had injuries that did not require lengthy hospitalization. Joseph Späh, after finding his family, told them he was unhurt. Only when his wife asked him why he was standing on one foot did he realize how much the other foot hurt. He had a fractured heel—his first broken bone after hundreds of falls during his career as an acrobat.

Ulla, the German shepherd, had been killed in the fire, but the Spähs told their children that she had survived and been found. Sure enough, a few days later, Späh produced a new Ulla, who became the family pet.

Peter Belin was not injured in his leap from the ship and was able to assist in rescuing others from the burning ship. Only after an hour or two of frantic activity did he remember that his parents had been waiting at the airfield. He went to the parking lot to search for their car, only to find it being slowly driven away, his parents believing him dead in the wreckage. Belin ran after the car, hopped on the side running board, and stuck his head in the window. His mother fainted.

Richard Kollmer, one of the four crewmen who had been nearest the source of the fire, was quickly able to send a telegram to his parents in Germany telling them he was safe. The Kollmers thus became one of the first people in that country to hear of the disaster since it occurred at about 1:30 A.M. German time.

REACTION IN GERMANY

As far as most Germans knew, the *Hindenburg* had landed safely. Captain Pruss's last radio message read, "Ready for landing in bad weather." An operator in Hamburg relayed the message "Hindenburg landed" to the Redeerei, and this was the message given to the official government news agency. This mistake would make the truth all the more of a shock.

Hugo Eckener was in Graz, Austria, having just made a speech in Vienna. The *New York Times* Berlin correspondent reached him there to break the news. At first, Eckener refused to believe it. But at last, his voice shaking with emotion, he said he was "shocked and very sorrowful for all on board."

Early the next morning, he flew to Berlin, where he seemed a "pathetic figure" to one of the reporters present, as quoted in Archbold's book *Hindenburg*. He immediately seized on sabotage as a possible explanation for the disaster. He told *New York Times* reporters that the Redeerei had received several threats, and that "it is just possible that one such threat materialized in the brain of some fanatic."

That was said, however, before he went to the Air Ministry for an interview with Hermann Göring. It would never do, Eckener was told, for people to think such an important symbol of Nazi power could be destroyed by the party's enemies. Another cause would have to be found. Göring also said, as quoted by Archbold, that, despite his personal dislike of airships, "now we *have* to persist in them."

AN ABOUT-FACE

Before he left for the United States, as the head of an investigations team appointed by Göring, Eckener told the *New York Times*, "A question of sabotage, I must confess, occurred to me in the first moment . . . but after the latest news [about weather conditions] only a very slight probability for this solution of the mystery remains." A moment later, he added, "Colonel General Goering . . . indefatigably holds fast to the idea of building airships . . . for this conviction we airship men have to thank the government of Adolf Hitler from the depths of our hearts."

German newspapers echoed the theme. As reported by the *New York Times*, the official German news service urged citizens to "stand up under the blow" and to look toward the LZ130 then under construction. The main headline of the *Lokalanzeiger* was "Forward, despite everything." Another newspaper, *Die Angriff*, proclaimed that while "the king of the air is dead; we will provide another king." Eckener's son, Kurt, speaking from the assembly plant in Friedrichshafen, predicted that the LZ130 would begin regular service to America in a few months.

TOWNS IN MOURNING

Other people in Friedrichshafen and in Zeppelinheim, the newly built village near Frankfurt where most of the crew members and their families lived, were more concerned about the present than the future. Lehmann's wife, Marie, had been one of the first to receive a predawn call with news of the disaster. She called Eleanore Pruss, and the two women began calling other family members of the crew. There was little to tell—only that the *Hindenburg* had burned and crashed, and that there was no word about survivors.

Many of the wives hurried to the Redeerei headquarters in Frankfurt, even though it was not yet open. When the clerks finally arrived, they were not able to provide much information. One woman, however, had an unusual request. Erich Spehl's girlfriend wanted to know how she could collect on an insurance policy she had taken out on him. The astounded clerk asked how she could know he was dead when no casualty list had been received.

Such a list was gradually forthcoming. The women waited patiently as news trickled in from New Jersey. The *New York Times* reported "heart-rending scenes" as relatives learned that their family members were alive and well; alive but injured; or dead. Alfred Bernhard's wife was not at the Redeerei. She was in the late stages of pregnancy, and the other women waited as long as possible before breaking the news to her that she was now a widow. In coming days, black crepe dresses and veils would become a common sight on the streets of Friedrich-shafen and Zeppelinheim.

Two survivors of the *Hindenburg* were Werner Franz *(left)* and Heinrich Kubis *(right)*. Franz was a cabin boy and Kubis served as chief steward. Working in the kitchen at the time of the disaster, the two managed an incredibly lucky escape from the fiery blaze.

The sorrow of these two towns was shared throughout the nation. Movie theaters in Berlin replaced comedies with more serious films. Radio stations played dirges instead of dance music. Churchgoers said prayers for the souls of the dead and the recovery of the injured. The *New York Times* reported that

Göring, speaking to the German Air Club, said, "A higher power, in a few minutes, destroyed what human hands by infinite care had constructed. We bow to God's will, and at the same time we face the future with an unbending will . . . to continue the work for the conquest of the air."

THE ZEPPELINS GROUNDED

That work, however, would be put on hold. The *Graf Zeppelin* landed at Flughafen on May 8, its crew and passengers shocked and somber at the news of what had happened to the *Hindenburg*. A day later, Göring ordered the ship grounded pending the outcome of an investigation of the fire. Shortly

The *Hindenburg*'s Sister Ship

As the *Hindenburg* lay burning in New Jersey, its sister ship, the *Graf Zeppelin*, was making the return trip to Germany from Argentina. It was early morning, and the ship was nearing the Canary Islands when a radio operator brought a bulletin about the disaster to Captain Hans von Schiller.

At first, Schiller did not believe it. He had been copied hours before on a message mistakenly reporting that the *Hindenburg* had landed. Only minutes later, however, a message came through from Frankfurt confirming the news.

"I thought it best under the circumstances to withhold it from others until 8 A.M. today [Saturday, May 8] when I told the crew," he was quoted in the *New York Times*. "The passengers were informed much later."

The *Graf Zeppelin* was ordered grounded by German air minister Hermann Göring shortly after landing at Frankfurt, and it never flew again.

afterward, Hitler decreed that neither the *Graf Zeppelin* nor the new LZ130 would fly until the question of helium versus hydrogen had been settled.

The Germans' caution was echoed in the United States. Two days after Hitler's order, the U.S. Army ordered its three airships deflated, even though they had been filled with helium. And the chairman of the U.S. Senate Military Affairs Committee gave his opinion that, in the future, airships would be used only for freight instead of passengers.

As the controversy continued, Eckener sailed for the United States to take part in the official inquiry. Part of that investigation was a thorough search of the crash site. Police officers, FBI agents, and Navy personnel looked through and around what *New York Times* reporter Russell Porter called "the once proud and handsome monarch of the air." It now resembled "the skeleton of some prehistoric reptilian monster." The fire had been so intense that there was little for them to find. Otto Clemens's blackened cameras turned up, as did the movie camera that had belonged to Joseph Späh. Also identifiable was the toy car that had been taken from Werner Doehner. Post office officials found remnants of letters, some of which could be cleaned and sent on their way.

SOUVENIRS

Among the investigators was Heinrich Bauer, the most senior officer still physically able to climb around the wreckage. At first, he saw nothing but the twisted Duralumin girders. Then, he spotted a flat object and brushed the ashes away to reveal a blackened silver serving platter carrying the Redeerei insignia. It would become his personal keepsake.

Bauer would not be the only person who wanted a souvenir of the *Hindenburg*. In the days immediately after the disaster, before a security system was implemented, fortune hunters plundered the wreck, carrying away pieces of burned metal or fabric that they would subsequently sell. Eventually, the base was closed to the public, and about 200 armed soldiers patrolled the perimeter with orders to shoot trespassers.

At least one person, however, was able to obtain a souvenir. On May 10, Rosendahl went to the site to find a guard trying to take a piece of scrap metal away from a young boy who spoke no English. The boy was Werner Franz, the cabin boy whose drenching with water probably saved his life. Rosendahl let him keep the metal piece.

The 28 Germans who lost their lives on the *Hindenburg* were given a memorial service on the pier of the Hamburg-America Line before being sent home. As word of the crash had filtered back to Germany, the wives of the crew members began to call each other with news and support. After receiving the casualty list, families began to wait for their loved ones' caskets to be sent overseas.

The security precautions did not keep the curious from getting as close as they could. During the week after the crash, the
roads around the Lakehurst area were jammed with onlookers,
many of whom had driven from neighboring states.

A WEEK OF FUNERALS

The week after the wreck was also marked with the funerals of
those who had died. The largest memorial service took place

"Don't Lose Faith"

In the days after the destruction of the *Hindenburg*, officials
in Germany and in the United States said repeatedly that,
despite the disaster, the building and flying of airships should
continue. Ambassador Hans Luther told the *New York Times*
about a plea supposedly made from Matilda Doehner, whose
husband and daughter had been killed:

> I shall never forget the words of a German lady passenger
> who was enroute to Mexico. Her husband was killed, but
> she doesn't know that yet. She saved her two small sons
> by literally throwing them out of the flaming ship. Her
> hands were badly burned by their clothing and she was
> otherwise critically injured. But, trying to smile, she said
> to me through swollen lips: "Herr Ambassador, don't lose
> confidence. Don't lose faith in Zeppelins."

The ambassador might not have known that Mrs. Doehner
had already hired an attorney to file suit against the Zeppelin
company.

on the pier of the Hamburg-America Line. A crowd estimated at 10,000 gathered in front of 28 coffins. An honor guard of brown- and white-shirted German Americans in paramilitary dress stood at attention behind the coffins, while the seats of honor were reserved for Heinrich Bauer and those surviving members of the crew well enough to attend. Eckener and his party had not yet arrived, but Ambassador Luther represented the German government.

After the singing of the "Horst Wessel" song and "Deutschland Über Alles," all the bodies except three were taken on board the *Hamburg* for the journey home. Journalist Birgir Brinck's body would go on a Swedish liner, and Feibusch's by ship to his native San Francisco. Lehmann's body awaited the arrival of his wife.

After arrival in the port city of Hamburg, the bodies were taken by special train to Frankfurt. Then, as the airport band that had seen them off so merrily just three weeks earlier played solemn hymns, they were placed in hearses. Six went to Friedrichshafen to be buried together under a marble headstone that read, as translated by Hoehling, "They have faithfully performed their duty, and will live wherever there are German airways."

Even as they mourned, the families of the 36 people whose lives had been lost probably could not help but wonder what exactly had happened to the *Hindenburg*. At Lakehurst, an investigative panel was trying to find an answer to that very question.

6 Investigation

Less than 24 hours after the *Hindenburg* crashed and burned, the U.S. Department of Commerce ordered an investigation. Assistant secretary J. Monroe Johnson, quoted in the *New York Times*, pledged that everything would be done to solve "a very, very puzzling situation." The *Times* also quoted Eckener as being confident that the inquiry would be conducted "with the utmost concentration and energy." But, however eager both the Americans and Germans were to get to the bottom of the disaster, there was one answer neither group wanted to find there—sabotage.

Eckener had received orders from air minister Hermann Göring to instruct the German witnesses to say nothing that would point toward sabotage, orders later confirmed in 1961 by surviving crewman German Zettel to author A.A. Hoehling. The United States, likewise, feared the embarrassment and international tension that would result if it were discovered that an American plot was responsible.

SPECULATION

There was no lack of people, however, who thought the *Hindenburg* had been sabotaged, and they did not hesitate to tell the

Federal Bureau of Investigation. Jews were frequent targets. One person claimed to have seen the ship fired on while flying over New York City. A letter sent to the FBI charged that "some hireling of anti-Nazis did this job and was paid by the Jews." A similar letter said, "Pure and Simple, it was an act of Jewish sabotage." And in Germany, rumors were spread that a cloud of smoke rising from the burning ship was shaped like a Jewish face.

After the tragedy, a three-man board gathered to confirm the cause of the fire. Using witness testimony and scientific experts, the inquest entertained several theories stating that the fire was caused by static electricity, equipment malfunction, and even sabotage.

Several people claimed to have seen something suspicious. One letter from New York City told of a small plane being attached by a rope to the *Hindenburg* as it flew over Manhattan. A New Jersey man wrote to the FBI about seeing three men "evidently waiting for the airship Hindenburg" in the Lakehurst area. One of them was "quickly hiding his rifle under his overcoat."

Yet another letter speculated that a time bomb had been planted aboard the ship before it left Germany—a theory still favored by some people. One man even claimed that Lehmann, with Eckener's knowledge, sabotaged the ship in order to eventually obtain helium. A bomb, the letter said, was timed to go off after the ship landed, but Lehmann had not counted on the long delay.

The FBI disregarded many of these letters. On one, an agent wrote a disparaging remark about "such nuts." Others, however, were checked out. After Ambassador Luther revealed the letter of warning from Kathie Rauch, an agent was sent to interview her and Georg Pfister. The agent's report said that while the pair seemed "hilariously exuberant over the fact that their visions had become true," he saw no reason to investigate further.

MORE SERIOUS THEORIES

In the days before the start of the investigation, however, more plausible theories were discussed. People assumed that the fire was caused when a mixture of hydrogen and air ignited. The questions were how the hydrogen escaped from a cell and what ignited the mixture.

A spark from static electricity, similar to the spark sometimes generated by a person touching a metal object such as a doorknob after walking on a carpet, was suggested as a source for the ignition. Airships always built up static electricity during their voyages, and the thunderstorms around Lakehurst just before the landing would have made conditions favorable for a greater-than-usual buildup. Grounding—some connection between the ship and the ground—would have been necessary to discharge the static electricity as a spark. Some experts thought that the mooring ropes dropped from the bow provided this grounding.

Dry manila ropes, however, would not conduct an electrical charge, but it was thought that perhaps the light rain had soaked the ropes to a point where conduction took place. Another suggestion was that the stream of water discharged from the ballast tanks to balance the ship provided the means of conduction.

Since sparks had been seen by some observers on the ground, it was proposed that when the diesel engines had been put into reverse to slow the *Hindenburg*, one or more engines backfired. The sparks coming from the engine, it was thought, might have ignited a mixture caused when hydrogen was valved off, expelled from the ship to bring it lower.

Another possibility involved a report that Captain Pruss, just prior to the fire, had ordered the stern mooring ropes to be "paid out," or extended from the ship, once they had been grasped by the ground crew. Some observers reported seeing the ship lurch to one side, as if the line on one side, but not the other, was paid out. The lurching, some said, might have caused the bottom fin of the *Hindenburg* to strike the ground, with the resulting friction setting off the sparks igniting the hydrogen-air mixture.

SABOTAGE PLAYED DOWN

One possible solution, however, received scant attention. The *New York Times* said that, while officials promised to consider sabotage, "both American and German official sources have discarded virtually all credence in stories that a rifleman might have shot a bullet into the ship, that the hydrogen tanks might have been slit to allow the gas to escape, and such tales."

At least one member of the crew, however, believed in the bullet theory. Some observers had said the initial plume of flame spurting from the top rear of the *Hindenburg* had a bluish cast. Captain Heinrich Bauer was convinced, as he later told author A.A. Hoehling, that a *leuchtspurteschoss*, or incendiary bullet, had been fired into the ship from the woods outside the landing field. He would share his views, however, only with his German comrades.

The investigation thus began with a host of competing theories. Although all were deemed possible, none drew firm support from scientists. Indeed, experts contacted by the *New York Times* said that, because the virtually total destruction of the ship would have destroyed all clues, they were "more or less resigned to a semi-negative outcome of the investigation."

THE HEARING BEGINS

Nevertheless, on the morning of May 10, the formal investigation began. The three-man board was chaired by South Trimble, the Commerce Department's chief attorney. There were three technical advisers, including Commander Rosendahl, plus potential witnesses and about 100 reporters and cameramen.

Rosendahl would be the first witness called. The Navy commander immediately cast doubt on the static electricity theory. He said that the handling of the mooring ropes by the landing crew would have grounded the *Hindenburg*, but he pointed out that the fire did not occur until about four minutes after the lines were dropped, more than enough time for all static electricity to have been discharged.

He also testified that, although there was some miscommunication between the *Hindenburg* and the ground crew as to the handling of the lines, the ship was about 150 feet above the ground at the time. "The Hindenburg did not touch the ground at any time until the fire brought her down," he said, according to the *New York Times*.

Rosendahl also addressed a report that the ship had made a sharp turn while approaching the mooring mast. Such a maneuver, he said, was "nothing unusual" and that ships filled with hydrogen must constantly "readjust their equilibrium and static position" while valving off gas. As to the basic cause of the disaster, he said, "I have no knowledge of what was the origin of the fire."

THE PROPELLER THEORY

After a day off to attend the memorial service, the investigation resumed. Navy lieutenant Benjamin May, who had been atop the mooring mast, suggested a new theory. He testified, the *New York Times* said, that "the side of the ship just aft of [behind] the rear [engine gondola] seemed to collapse outward." At the same time, he said, he heard a "cracking" sound, possibly made by a piece of propeller blade smashing through the hull of the ship after breaking away from the engine.

That afternoon, board members adjourned to make an inspection of the wreck. When they reconvened, they announced that two small pieces of wooden propeller blade had been found near the edge of the burned ship and that experts would be called on analyze the pieces.

Lieutenant May and another witness, Lieutenant Raymond Tyler, also disagreed with Rosendahl that the ship was grounded. The *New York Times* quoted Tyler as saying that the manila ropes, when they hit the ground, were so dry that they raised a "cloud of dust" and thus could not have discharged the static electricity.

On Thursday, May 13, two members of the ground crew told the board about having noticed something wrong with the vertical rudders of the *Hindenburg*. The lower rudder, they said, was turned hard to the left while the upper was straight, when ideally they should have been turned the same way. In addition, Navy chief boatswain's mate Fred Tobin testified, as quoted in the *New York Times*, that he saw what he described as broken cable that "thrashed around" the tail of the ship. No explanation was given as to how this could have ignited the fire.

ECKENER ARRIVES

Late that night, the ship bearing Eckener and the German delegation docked in New York City. Early the next morning, they went to Lakehurst to view the wreckage. According to Hoehling's book, one reporter noted tears on Eckener's cheeks and heard him murmur, in German, "Sad, sad." Pressed for an opinion, he said only, according to the *New York Times*, that, so long as the inquiry continued, it would be impossible

Sabotage?

Although most of the *Hindenburg*'s crew, as ordered, dismissed all talk of sabotage, many believed that was the cause of the airship's destruction. Certainly, this was true of Anton Witteman, who was observed signaling sanctioned answers to some of his colleagues.

Interviewed by A.A. Hoehling for the book *Who Destroyed the Hindenburg?*, Witteman said there was no way that either lightning or bullets could have downed the ship. He said that, throughout his 25 years of experience, his ships had been hit by lightning, bullets, and shell fragments many times without serious damage. Furthermore, he said, the lines dropped from the ship were too dry to have grounded it, leading to a static electricity discharge.

"There is no doubt," he concluded, "that the cause of the *Hindenburg* catastrophe is sabotage."

for him to give "any statement or any ideas regarding the causes of the disaster."

The German delegation attended the investigation for the first time later that day. Eckener took an active role, taking notes and passing along suggested questions to the panel members. He may have already passed along orders to say nothing that could point toward sabotage. One of the witnesses, chief steward Kubis, testified that passengers were never allowed into the interior of the ship without an escort, but he said nothing about exceptions he knew had taken place.

The next two days provided some of the most important testimony, as Freund, Lau, and Sauter—three of the men who had been closest to the fire—took the stand. Freund said his first impression had been that a gas cell had exploded and that he saw or heard nothing that would indicate a structural failure or something tearing through the side of the ship.

Sauter was the first witness to pinpoint the source of the fire as gas cell No. 4, but he was reluctant to offer any more information. He seemed to hesitate before answering questions, and reporters noticed that he was looking across the room at Captain Anton Witteman, who either nodded or shook his head depending on the question. Chairman Trimble noticed, too, and ruled that witnesses would no longer be allowed in the hearing room until it was their turn to testify.

Sauter did say, however, that he could think of no way that sparks from the engine could have gotten into the ship's interior. He also said that gas that had been valved off would have been sucked out of vents at the top of the ship and could not have descended to the engines.

THE SECRET INVESTIGATION

Lau's testimony that he saw the fire start inside cell No. 4 apparently took the German delegation by surprise. According to Hoehling's book, they spoke excitedly among themselves as Eckener took notes. Hoehling also wrote that the German

One of the duties of the *Hindenburg* investigative board was to look for evidence of sabotage. Two men, Erich Spehl and Joseph Späh, became persons of interest as descriptions of their suspicious behavior and strange recollections of the tragedy were told to authorities.

delegation and officers then began holding late-night meetings among themselves, conducting their own, private examination while briefing crew members on what they should and should not say during official questioning.

In the days that followed, the various theories were examined in detail. Most were found to be implausible. Sauter's doubts about the valved-off hydrogen were echoed by Bauer, who testified that he had followed standard procedure by releasing the gas in time for it to dissipate long before the engines were reversed.

The propeller theory was discarded after it was learned that spare propeller blades were stored only about 150 feet from where the fire broke out. In addition, an expert who had examined a piece found in the wreck said that, in his opinion, the propeller from which it had come broke on contact with the ground, not in the air. In other testimony, the supposedly broken cable was shown to be part of the lower rudder's rigging.

Two possibilities for the cause of an electric spark near No. 4—an impulse from the ship's radio or a short circuit in the instrument used to measure the bag's pressure—were discussed and discarded. The German delegation even suggested that a high-frequency radio beam used at Lakehurst could have been the cause. But an expert was called who testified that the beam had so tiny an electrical output— "less than one flypower" as quoted in the *New York Times*—that it could not have done any damage.

Other types of electrical discharges were proposed, such as ball lightning—a glowing sphere of electricity sometimes seen in connection with thunderstorms—and St. Elmo's fire—an electrical discharge during which the surrounding atmosphere glows from ionization. At the time, no one mentioned seeing either phenomenon, but years later a witness, according to Rick Archbold's *Hindenburg*, told of seeing St. Elmo's fire "flickering along the airship's back a full minute before the fire broke out."

ECKENER'S TESTIMONY

Finally, on May 21, Eckener took the stand. He rejected all ideas of sabotage, saying there was no evidence to support any of them. His personal belief, he said, was that the sharp turn of the *Hindenburg* described by some witnesses had possibly resulted in the breaking of one of the shear wires bracing the rudder. The loose wire could have ripped gas cell No. 4, causing the cell to lose enough hydrogen to mix with the air under the outer cover and cause the "rippling" effect noticed by Lieutenant Antrim. The mixture, he said, according to the *New York Times*, was then ignited by St. Elmo's fire or static electricity. Eckener was careful to say that he did not necessarily believe this was what happened, only that he considered it the most plausible given all the facts.

But, even though Eckener's theory was supported by Professor Max Deickmann of the German delegation, an American professor of electrical engineering, Dr. John Whitehead of Johns Hopkins University, subsequently testified, according to the *Times*, that "there is nothing whatsoever to support the theory or belief that the disaster had its origin in any electrostatic discharge . . . in any form."

ROSENDAHL'S DOUBTS

Meanwhile, Rosendahl, who had joined all others in publicly rejecting sabotage, was having second thoughts. On the evening of May 18, only one day after he was quoted in the news media discounting the idea of sabotage, he called the FBI to request a meeting. Accordingly, special agents W.S. Devereaux and Lee Malone went to Lakehurst.

According to Devereaux's memorandum to FBI director J. Edgar Hoover, Rosendahl said that Eckener had confided to him that, despite his many comments to the contrary, he believed that the *Hindenburg* "met her ill-timed fate due to the employment of sabotage, either on the part of Communists or on the part of sympathizers with the Anti-Nazi movement."

Rosendahl added that he shared Eckener's opinion. He had been convinced by Lau's testimony of seeing a glow inside cell No. 4. Furthermore, Rosendahl told the FBI about the Germans' private investigation, including the information about Joseph Späh's unauthorized visits to the ship's interior. The Navy commander said that both he and members of the German delegation now believed that Späh, employing his agility as an acrobat, had climbed up the shaft between cells No. 4 and

5 and planted "either an inflammable substance . . . or placed a timing device which would have ignited the mixture."

THE GERMAN MEMO

Soon after this meeting, Eckener's group sent a confidential memo to the investigating panel. In it, according to an FBI report, the possibility of sabotage was thoroughly discussed. The conclusion was that the most likely cause would have been a bomb or some other incendiary device placed aboard the ship either before it left Frankfurt or by a passenger during flight. The Germans steadfastly refused to entertain the possibility that a crew member had set such a device.

On July 21, Rosendahl sent a private memorandum to the investigating committee. It said, as quoted by Hoehling, that "the simplest way of having sabotaged the ship would have been to place in the gas cell trunk a device with some sort of time element, of course, which would cause flame to be propagated into the gas cells."

On the same day, however, the Department of Commerce committee issued its final report. As given in FBI files, it said that a leak "in the vicinity of cells 4 and 5 caused a combustible mixture to form in the upper stern part of the ship. . . . The theory that a brush discharge [St. Elmo's fire] ignited such a mixture appears most probable."

Rosendahl was not satisfied. He wrote to the committee chairman, as quoted by Hoehling, that "I feel it is just as much justification for assigning sabotage as a probable cause as there is of . . . St. Elmo's fire."

PRAISE IN GERMANY

However, Eckener, now back in Germany, praised the report. It was for the most part the same as the public report he and his colleagues had turned in to Göring's Air Ministry. That report listed eight possible causes, including sabotage, but said, according to Hoehling's book, "no completely certain proof can be found for any of the possibilities cited above."

But if the *Hindenburg* was sabotaged, as Rosendahl and Eckener both strongly suspected, who could have done it? Security had been extraordinarily tight at Frankfurt, and the

Suspect Joseph Späh

On May 24, after Joseph Späh came under scrutiny by the FBI, he received a letter from the investigating board asking him for his recollections of what had happened. This excerpt from his answering letter is found in the FBI files on the *Hindenburg* case:

I was at the time of the first Explosion, on the window furthest up toward the Nose of the Ship, in the Diningroom, facing the Hangar, taking a photograph of the Groundcrew. With the suddenness of the whole thing, there was no time for me to observe just where the whole thing was happening or where it started from, from the way we were rising for a second and from the reflection of the explosion on the ground, I could imagine that we had gone up in flames, I jumped out from a great height and when I landed on the ground ran off without looking back, thus at no time did I see any flames, nor do I have the slightest idea, nor could I have, toward the solution of the accident.

The FBI conducted an investigation of Späh but dropped him as a suspect after uncovering no motive and receiving only excellent reports on his character.

chance of an unauthorized person slipping aboard unnoticed seemed slight.

The FBI concentrated on Joseph Späh. He was known to have made unaccompanied visits inside the ship, and the fact that he lived in the United States but traveled under a foreign passport seemed suspicious. However, he did not seem to have had a motive for sabotage beyond a vague mention in an FBI memo that a crewman has reported that Späh "seemed to him to be unsympathetic to airship travel."

Nevertheless, Special Agent Malone conducted an investigation of Späh. He found nothing suspicious. Indeed, he reported that "Späh was considered by all who knew him to bear an excellent reputation."

THE CASE AGAINST SPEHL

In his book *Who Destroyed the Hindenburg?*, Hoehling accuses Erich Spehl, the young rigger. He suggests that Spehl's girlfriend and her leftist, perhaps Communist, friends might have convinced him to destroy the ship as an anti-Nazi statement.

If Spehl, indeed, had a motive for sabotage, he certainly also had an opportunity. As a rigger, he moved freely about the interior of the ship and could have, at almost any time, planted a device in a fold of gas cell No. 4 or even within the cell itself. Hoehling theorized that Spehl either made a mistake in setting the time or that the device malfunctioned.

The device, Hoehling suggests, could have consisted of a dry-cell battery, a flashbulb, and a timer. Spehl had ready access to such equipment as an amateur photographer. It would have been possible for him to have scratched the surface of the bulb so that it would explode when charged, thus releasing the pure oxygen inside. The heat of the bulb—about 6,400°F—would have been more than enough to ignite the oxygen-hydrogen mixture.

Sauter, in fact, had compared the sound he heard to a flashbulb. And Hoehling also cited a letter to Rosendahl on

The first memorial service for the *Hindenburg* was held shortly after the tragedy *(above)*. A commemorative service is held every year for survivors and their family members at the Lakehurst Naval Air Station in New Jersey. In 2007, one of the last living survivors, Werner Doehner, attended the 70th anniversary of the tragedy. Doehner was one of the *Hindenburg*'s youngest passengers; he survived by being thrown out a window of the burning dirigible.

May 29 from the Bureau of Explosives of the Association of American Railroads. The bureau's chief chemist had analyzed a small substance found at the crash site by the New York City bomb squad. The substance, the chemist reported, "is probably the insoluble residue from the depolarizing element of a small dry battery"—the kind strictly prohibited on board the ship.

In researching his book, Hoehling brought up Spehl's name in interviews with several *Hindenburg* survivors. Their replies were vague and noncommittal. Even years after the disaster, they refused to believe one of their crewmates could have been responsible.

NEW EVIDENCE

To the public, the *Hindenburg* disaster remained a complete mystery. The Redeerei, however, was soon to have a much better idea of what might have happened. Company officials in 1937 asked electrical engineer Otto Beyersdorf to run tests on fragments of the gas cells, which had been coated with a reflective substance. Beyersdorf reported, as quoted in the National Hydrogen Association's online newsletter, that the "actual cause of the fire was the extreme easy flammability of the covering material brought about by discharges of an electrostatic nature." The findings were not made public at the time, but the makeup of the coating was altered for the LZ130 then under construction.

Beyersdorf's letter was found and translated in 1997 by Addison Bain, an engineer who was retired from the National Aeronautics and Space Administration. Bain also was able to run tests on a fragment from one of the *Hindenburg*'s gas cells and found it to contain both cellulose nitrate and aluminum powder. Bain replicated Beyersdorf's tests and got the same result. Even after 60 years, a piece of the fabric ignited and burned when subjected to electric shock.

Questions still remain. Bain's theory has its critics, just as all the other theories that preceded it. Other theories as to what turned the *Hindenburg* from a majestic symbol of power to a flaming wreck may come forward. If none can be proved, then, as Hugo Eckener told the *New York Times*, "the whole thing must be regarded as a mystery."

7 Das Ende

When a passenger shouted just before the crash that it was *Das Ende*, or "The End," he could have been speaking for the airship industry as well as for the *Hindenburg*. Although Rosendahl in the United States and Eckener in Germany tried their best to keep Count Zeppelin's dream alive, the era of the passenger airship ended at Lakehurst. One more zeppelin would fly, but not for long and never with passengers. And dirigibles still can be seen, but they are pale shadows of what once was.

The success of the Redeerei depended on whether it could obtain helium from the United States. Eckener did his best to take advantage of the shock over the loss of so many lives aboard the *Hindenburg* to get the embargo overturned. He met with favorable responses, and the Helium Control Act was amended to permit export for nonmilitary uses.

Before such an export could take place for the new LZ130, however, Nazi Germany annexed its neighbor Austria. Anti-German feeling in the United States ran so high that, even as a German ship waited to take on the first cargo of helium, U.S. Secretary of the Interior Harold Ickes refused to release it.

THE ECONOMIC FACTOR

Even if the Redeerei had obtained helium, it might not have made a difference. A helium ship might be safer, but it was not as profitable. Besides costing more than twice as much as hydrogen, helium lacked hydrogen's lifting power. Consequently, the LZ130 would have been able to accommodate only 40 passengers to the *Hindenburg*'s 72. To make the voyage profitable, ticket prices might have been too high for all but the most wealthy travelers.

As the years went on, the surviving crew of the *Hindenburg* *(above)* would do their best to meet at the annual *Hindenburg* memorial at Lakehurst Naval Air Station in New Jersey.

Economic factors aside, however, the days of the large, passenger airship were numbered. The evolution of the airship had reached a dead end. There was no practical way to make airships large enough to meet passenger demand or fast enough to compete with the steadily improving transoceanic service offered by airlines.

The LZ30 would be completed with great fanfare and christened the *Graf Zeppelin II* on September 14, 1938. With Eckener in command, it flew 30 "demonstration" flights over the next year, most of them either for propaganda or spy missions. But, with the outbreak of World War II, Göring took the opportunity to dispense with the airships he had despised all along. He ordered both *Graf Zeppelins* demolished and their metal frames recycled as airplanes. The huge hangars at Frankfurt were dynamited.

THE NEW ZEPPELIN COMPANY

The count's company, however, still exists in Friedrichshafen under the name Zeppelin-Metalwerk, although it has not built a zeppelin since 1938. Its products now include metal objects from tractors to radio antennae. Each year on May 7, a ceremony is held to remember the *Hindenburg* and those who died in the disaster. Many survivors have attended. In 1987, 50 years after the fire and crash, four crewmen remained—Hans König, Werner Franz, Richard Kollmer, and Xavier Maier. In 2007, only one remained—Franz, the cabin boy whose life was saved by a ruptured water tank. The only surviving passenger was Werner Doehner, the boy who had to surrender his toy car.

All the rest are gone. Erich Spehl's mysterious girlfriend, according to various versions, went to the Soviet Union during the war and never returned; she made her home in Switzerland, or maybe she remained in Frankfurt where she was shunned by women whose husbands had been lost on the *Hindenburg*. Charles Rosendahl received a Navy Cross as commander of the U.S.S. *Minneapolis* in World War II before returning to airships. He retired as an admiral and died in 1977.

Hugo Eckener would not give up believing in the airship. In 1946, he came to the United States as an adviser on a project to build a dirigible 950 feet long and filled with helium. The plan died when neither private nor government funding could be found.

Eckener returned to Germany for good, spending most of his remaining years writing his autobiography. He died in 1954 and is buried under the marble memorial at Friedrichshafen, joining six of "his boys." Shortly before his death, he finally admitted to author Harold G. Dick in *Graf Zeppelin and Hindenburg,* "The zeppelin has given way to the airplane; a good thing has been replaced by a better."

Chronology

1852	**September 24:** Henri Giffard, in France, makes first dirigible flight.
1863	Count von Zeppelin takes first balloon flight near St. Paul, Minnesota.
1890	Count von Zeppelin resigns from the army; he devotes time to building airships.
1900	**July 2:** First flight of zeppelin LZ1
1908	**August 5:** LZ4 wrecked; German people support the building of more airships.

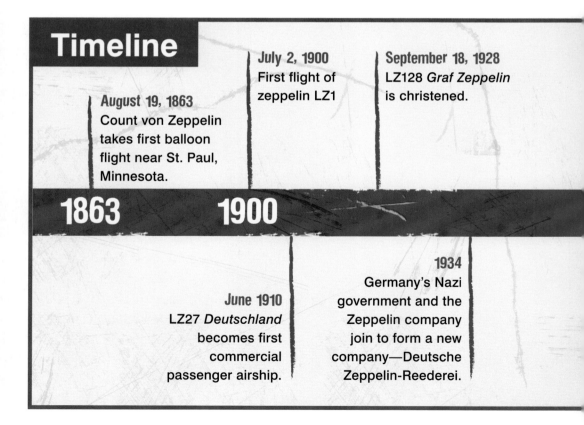

Timeline

August 19, 1863
Count von Zeppelin takes first balloon flight near St. Paul, Minnesota.

July 2, 1900
First flight of zeppelin LZ1

September 18, 1928
LZ128 *Graf Zeppelin* is christened.

1863

1900

June 1910
LZ27 *Deutschland* becomes first commercial passenger airship.

1934
Germany's Nazi government and the Zeppelin company join to form a new company—Deutsche Zeppelin-Reederei.

1910	**June:** LZ7 *Deutschland* becomes the first commercial passenger airship.
1914–1918	World War II spurs advancements in zeppelin technology.
1917	**March 8:** Count von Zeppelin dies.
1922	Germany renews airship construction, building LZ126 *Los Angeles* for the U.S. Navy.
1928	**September 18:** LZ127 *Graf Zeppelin* is christened.
1929	**August 29:** *Graf Zeppelin* completes a voyage around the world.

March 4, 1936
LZ129 *Hindenburg* makes first flight.

May 11, 1937
German Chancellor Adolf Hitler grounds German airship fleet.

1937

May 6, 1937
Hindenburg catches fire, crashes at Lakehurst Naval Air Station, in New Jersey.

July 23, 1937
Investigating committee issues report citing hydrogen leakage, static electricity as probable cause.

1934	Germany's Nazi government and the Zeppelin company join to form a new company—Deutsche Zeppelin-Reederei
1936	**March 4:** LZ129 *Hindenburg* makes first flight.
	May 6: *Hindenburg* begins first flight to United States.
1937	**May 3:** *Hindenburg* departs from Germany on final flight.
	May 6: *Hindenburg* catches fire, crashes at Lakehurst Naval Air Station, in New Jersey.
	May 10: Official U.S. Commerce Department investigation begins into cause of *Hindenburg* disaster.
	May 11: German Chancellor Adolf Hitler grounds German airship fleet.
	May 18: U.S. Navy Commander Charles Rosendahl contacts the FBI about possibility of sabotage.
	May 21: Hugo Eckener, head of Deutsche Zeppelin-Reederei, testifies before investigating committee.
	July 23: Investigating committee issues report citing hydrogen leakage, static electricity as probable cause.

Glossary

aft   Toward the rear of a ship or aircraft.

ballast   Something heavy, like bags of sand or water, that can be dropped to control the altitude of a dirigible or balloon.

bow   The front of a ship or aircraft.

buoyant   Tending to float or rise.

deluge   A great flood of water; a drenching.

detonation   An explosion.

dirigible   An airship capable of being controlled or steered.

forward   Toward the front of a ship or aircraft.

gestapo   Short for *Geheime Staatspolezei*, or "Secret State Police."

hearse   A vehicle for conveying a dead person to the place of burial.

incendiary   Used or adapted for setting something on fire.

Luftwaffe   German air force.

manifest   A list of the cargo carried by a ship.

promenade   An area used for walking.

propaganda   The spreading of information or images reflecting the views and interests of those advocating a particular point of view or cause.

reconnaissance   An organized search for useful military information.

St. Elmo's Fire   An electrical weather phenomenon in which flickering light is created by a discharge originating from a grounded object in an atmospheric electricity field.

stern   The rear of a ship or aircraft.

tether   To tie down, or the rope or chain by which something is secured.

yaw   A deviation from a straight course to one side or the other.

zeppelin   Any of the dirigible airships built by the company founded by Count von Zeppelin.

Bibliography

Adelt, Leonhard. "The Last Trip of the Hindenburg." *Reader's Digest*, November 1937, pp. 69–72.

Archbold, Rick. *Hindenburg*. Toronto: Madison Press Books, 2005.

Bokow, Jacquelyn Cochran. "Hydrogen Exonerated in Hindenburg Disaster." *National Hydrogen Association News* 2, no. 2 (Spring 1997). Available online. URL: http://www.hydrogenassociation.org/advocate/ad22zepp.htm. Downloaded on September 11, 2007.

Brantley, Dwight. Letter to J. Edgar Hoover, June 8, 1943. "The Hindenburg Disaster." Federal Bureau of Investigation. Available online. URL: http://foia.fbi.gov/foiaindex/hindburg.htm. Downloaded on August 29, 2007.

"Burns Are Fatal to Capt. Lehmann." *New York Times*, May 8, 1937, p. 1.

"Career of Captain Lehmann a Dedication to Vision of the Airship." *New York Times*, May 8, 1937, p. 2.

Courtney, W.B. "Sky Cruise." *Collier's*, May 8, 1937.

"Critical Paper Is Seized." *New York Times*, May 16, 1937, p. 13.

"Deaths Rise to 36; 8 on Critical List." *New York Times*, May 9, 1937, p. 30.

De Syon, Guillaume. *Zeppelin!: Germany and the Airship, 1900–1939*. Baltimore: Johns Hopkins University Press, 2002.

Devereaux, W.S. Memorandum to J. Edgar Hoover, May 19, 1937. "The Hindenburg Disaster." Federal Bureau of Investigation. Available online. URL: http://foia.fbi.gov/foiaindex/hindburg.htm. Downloaded on August 29, 2007.

DiChristina, Mariette. "What Really Downed the Hindenburg." *Popular Science*, November 1997, pp. 71–76.

Dick, Harold G., and Douglas H. Robinson. *Graf Zeppelin and Hindenburg*. Washington, D.C.: Smithsonian Institution Press, 1985.

"Disaster Ascribed to Gas by Experts." *New York Times*, May 7, 1937, p. 1.

Donegan, T.J. "Destruction of Airship 'Hindenburg': Summary Report, February 24, 1938. "The Hindenburg Disaster." Federal Bureau of Investigation. Available online. URL: http://foia.fbi.gov/foiaindex/hindburg.htm. Downloaded on August 29, 2007.

"Eckener Arrives for Crash Inquiry." *New York Times*, May 14, 1937, p. 3.

"Eckener Flies to Berlin." *New York Times*, May 8, 1937, p. 4.

"Eckener Grieves Over Loss of Ship." *New York Times*, May 7, 1937, p. 18.

"Eckener to Sail for Inquiry Here." *New York Times*, May 8, 1937, p. 4.

"Germany Shocked by Tragedy." *New York Times*, May 7, 1937, p. 1.

"Göering Grateful for U.S. Rescue Work." *New York Times*, May 8, 1937, p. 4.

"Graf Zeppelin Home, Disaster News Withheld." *New York Times*, May 9, 1937, p. 30.

"Hindenburg Disaster." Electricinca. Available online. URL: http://www.electricinca.com/56/annotations/objects/hindenburg.pdf. Downloaded on September 17, 2007.

"Hitler Prohibits Hydrogen Flights." *New York Times*, May 12, 1937, p. 2.

Hoehling, A.A. *Who Destroyed the Hindenburg?* New York: Popular Library, 1962.

Kieran, Leo. "Dirigible Touches Ground in Landing." *New York Times*, May 9, 1937, p. 21.

"Lehmann Wrote Views on Airships." *New York Times*, May 9, 1937, p. 31.

Lobel, Louis. "Destruction of Airship 'Hindenburg,' Synopsis of Facts, June 17, 1937. "The Hindenburg Disaster." Federal Bureau of Investigation. Available online. URL: http://foia.fbi.gov/foiaindex/hindburg.htm. Downloaded on August 29, 2007.

"Luther Lauds Injured." New York Times, May 9, 1937, p. 31.

Mather, Margaret. "I Was on the Hindenburg." *Harper's Monthly Magazine*, November, 1937, pp. 590–595.

McAlister, Roy. *The Philosopher Mechanic*. Knowledge Publications, 2007.

Mooney, Michael. *The Hindenburg*. New York: Dodd, Mead, 1972.

"New Airships Due." *New York Times*, May 8, 1937, p. 1.

O'Laughlin, Herbert. "Passenger Tells of Escape Jump." *New York Times*, May 7, 1937, p. 18.

Porter, Russell B. "Airship's Rudders Awry, Two Testify." *New York Times*, May 14, 1937, p. 3.

Porter, Russell B. "Cause Is a Mystery." *New York Times*, May 8, 1937, p. 1.

Porter, Russell B. "Dr. Eckener Views Airship Wreckage." *New York Times*, May 15, 1937, p. 5.

Porter, Russell B. "Eckener Lays Airship Fire to Static and Leaking Gas." *New York Times*, May 23, 1937, p. 1.

Porter, Russell B. "Hazard of Sparks Feared on Airship." *New York Times*, May 21, 1937, p. 3.

Porter, Russell B. "Hindenburg Board Scans New Theory." *New York Times*, May 13, 1937, p. 22.

Porter, Russell B. "Hindenburg Freed Hydrogen 4 Times." *New York Times*, May 20, 1937, p. 12.

Porter, Russell B. "Hindenburg Rigger Tells of a Blast." *New York Times*, May 18, 1937, p. 3.

Porter, Russell B. "New Static Theory for Dirigible Fire." *New York Times*, May 25, 1937, p. 3.

Porter, Russell B. "Rosendahl Is Mystified by the Hindenburg Fire; Advised Captain to Land." *New York Times*, May 26, 1937, p. 1.

Porter, Russell B. "3 in Airship Fix Point of Blast." *New York Times*, May 19, 1937, p. 3.

Porter, Russell B. "Two Reject Static as Disaster Cause." *New York Times*, May 9, 1937, p. 2.

Porter, Russell B. "Wreckage Viewed." *New York Times*, May 9, p. 1.

"Report of Airship 'Hindenburg' Accident Investigation," *Air Commerce Bulletin*, U.S. Department of Commerce, August 15, 1937. "The Hindenburg Disaster." Federal Bureau of Investigation. Available online. URL: http://foia.fbi.gov/foiaindex/hindburg.htm. Downloaded on August 29, 2007.

"Ship Official Died Trying to Save Wife." *New York Times*, May 8, 1937, p. 3.

Späh, Joseph. Letter to Bureau of Air Commerce Investigation Board. "The Hindenburg Disaster." Federal Bureau of Investigation. Available online. URL: http://foia.fbi.gov/foiaindex/hindburg.htm. Downloaded on August 29, 2007.

Thompson, Craig. "Airship Like a Giant Torch on Darkening Jersey Field." *New York Times*, May 7, 1937, p. 1.

"3 Countries Honor Hindenburg Dead." *New York Times*, May 12, p. 1.

Further Reading

Archbold, Rick. *Hindenburg.* Toronto: Madison Press Books, 2005. Well-written account of Count Zeppelin's development of the airship and of the last flight of the *Hindenburg.* Illustrated beautifully by Ken Marschall.

De Angelis, Gina. *The Hindenburg.* New York: Chelsea House, 2000. Well-researched account of the Hindenburg with special detail to the aftereffects it had on air travel.

Gare Maritime. "Sky Cruise." Available online. URL: http://www. garemaritime.com/features/hindenburg. The Gare Maritime Web site is devoted to the history of travel, and this section includes much *Hindenburg* material, including a photo gallery.

Majoor, Muriel. *Inside the Hindenburg.* Boston: Little, Brown, 2000. Even though this is for younger readers, the wonderful illustrations by Ken Marschall give a vivid portrayal of the construction and layout of the *Hindenburg.*

Navy Lakehurst Historical Society. "Hindenburg (LZ-129)." Available online. URL: http://www.nlhs.com/hindenburg.htm. Excellent photographic history of the construction and short career of the *Hindenburg.*

Old Time Radio—Radio Days: A Soundbite History. "Radio Days–Hindenburg," Available online. URL: http://www.otr.com/hindenburg.shtml. This account of Herb Morrison's historic broadcast of the *Hindenburg* disaster includes an audio file of the entire broadcast.

Vidacom. "The Hindenburg Disaster—Titanic of the Sky." Available online. URL: http://www.vidicom-tv.com/tohiburg.htm. Short account of the *Hindenburg* disaster is accompanied by excellent newsreel footage of the fire and crash.

Picture Credits

Page:

Index

About the Author

WILLIAM W. LACE is a native of Fort Worth, Texas, where he is executive assistant to the chancellor at Tarrant County College. He holds a bachelor's degree from Texas Christian University, a master's degree from East Texas State University, and a doctorate from the University of North Texas. Prior to joining Tarrant County College, he was director of the News Service at the University of Texas at Arlington and a sportswriter and columnist for the *Fort Worth Star-Telegram*. He has written more than 40 nonfiction books for young readers on subjects ranging from the atomic bomb to the Dallas Cowboys. He and his wife, Laura, a retired school librarian, live in Arlington, Texas, and have two children and four grandchildren.